Classified
Document

Time Block Like a Pro!

T.D. Errol

Time Block Like A Pro!

T.D. Errol

Time Block Like A Pro!

By T.D. Errol

Copyright © 2024 by T.D. Errol
All rights reserved. No part of this book may be reproduced or transmitted in any form or by any means, electronic or mechanical, including photocopying, recording, or any information storage and retrieval system, without the publisher's prior written permission, except where permitted by law.

Published by Errol Publishing

This is a work of nonfiction. Names, characters, businesses, places, events, and incidents are either the products of the author's imagination or used in a fictitious manner. Any resemblance to actual persons, living or dead, or events is coincidental.

Cover Design by Clifford Daiss
Edited by Clifford Daiss

First Edition: September, 2024

ISBN: 9798339561439
Imprint: Independently published

Printed in the United States of America

Disclaimer

The information in this book is provided with the understanding that the author and

publisher are not rendering professional advice or services to the individual reader. The contents of this book are for informational purposes only and should not be used as a substitute for professional advice.

T.D. Errol Author Bio

T.D. Errol, an author and adventurer from Colorado, combines a love for the outdoors with a deep expertise in quality management and Six Sigma principles. A former U.S. Marine Corps infantry soldier, T.D. has channeled the discipline and resilience from military service into a successful career focused on leadership, continuous improvement, and personal growth.

With experience in quality standards, T.D. has become a respected voice in the field, offering valuable insights on achieving excellence across industries. Through his writing, T.D. empowers others to harness the power of Six Sigma methodologies to drive success and elevate performance. His work reflects a commitment to helping readers develop the skills needed to navigate the complexities of modern business and personal development.

In *Time Block Like a Pro!* and other works, T.D. shares practical wisdom and strategies, inspiring readers to reach their full potential while focusing on quality in everything they do.

Forward

The pressure to achieve more in less time has never been greater in today's fast-paced world. Distractions are plentiful, demands on our time are relentless, and the line between work and personal life has blurred. Amid this chaos, one principle stands out as a beacon of clarity and productivity: time blocking.

Time Block Like A Pro! is not just another book on time management. It is a guide to transforming how you approach your day, work, and life. Through time blocking, you will discover how to reclaim control of your schedule, focus on what truly matters, and achieve more with less stress.

The concept of time blocking may seem simple, even intuitive. Dividing your day into dedicated segments for specific tasks makes sense. However, as you will learn in this book, time blocking is more than a scheduling technique. It is a powerful personal and professional growth tool to help you align your daily actions with your most important goals.

The beauty of time blocking lies in its flexibility and adaptability. Whether you are a student juggling classes and assignments, a professional managing multiple projects, a parent balancing family and career, or someone striving to be available for personal passions, time blocking can suit your unique needs. This book offers many strategies, tools, and real-life examples to help you design a time-blocking system that works for you, regardless of your role or responsibilities.

As someone who has witnessed the transformative impact of time blocking firsthand, I can attest to its effectiveness. It is not just about getting more done but about getting the right things done. It is about finding balance, reducing overwhelm, and making intentional choices with your time. This book will guide you through the process, showing you how to create time blocks that maximize your productivity, maintain your focus, and enhance your overall well-being.

But this journey is not just about improving efficiency; it is about reclaiming your life. Time blocking encourages you to be present in each moment, whether working on a high-priority project, spending time with loved ones, or simply taking care of yourself. It reminds you that your time is valuable and how you spend it shapes your future.

As you embark on this journey, I encourage you to embrace the principles and practices shared in this book with an open mind and a willingness to experiment. Time blocking is a skill that can be refined over time, and its benefits will only grow as you continue to apply and adapt it to your life.

Time Block Like A Pro! is more than a manual; it is an invitation to take control of your time and, in doing so, take control of your life. I am excited for you to discover the power of time blocking and the positive changes it can bring to your productivity, balance, and overall sense of fulfillment.

Here is to your success!

T.D.

Contents

Introduction	9
Chapter 1: Understanding Time Blocking	14
Chapter 2: Getting Started with Time Blocking	21
Chapter 3: Designing Your Time Blocks	29
Chapter 4: Tools and Techniques for Time Blocking	37
Chapter 5: Implementing Time Blocking in Daily Life	47
Chapter 6: Overcoming Challenges with Time Blocking	52
Chapter 7: Advanced Time Blocking Strategies	58
Chapter 8: Case Studies and Success Stories	64
Chapter 9: Adapting Time Blocking Over Time	68
Conclusion	74
Appendices	77

Introduction

The Power of Time Blocking:

Time blocking is a powerful technique that has the potential to revolutionize how we approach our daily tasks, both personally and professionally. It is more than just a scheduling method; it is a philosophy of intentional time management that brings structure, focus, and discipline to our often chaotic and fragmented lives. By assigning specific blocks of time to particular tasks or activities, time blocking helps us prioritize what truly matters, minimize distractions, and achieve higher productivity.

At its core, time blocking is about reclaiming control over our most valuable resource: time. In a world filled with constant demands and distractions, it is easy to fall into the trap of reactive work, where urgent but not necessarily important tasks dictate our days. Time blocking, however, allows us to proactively plan our days, aligning our actions with our goals and values. This method shifts our mindset from simply getting through the day to making the day work for us.

The science behind time management reveals that humans are not naturally wired to multitask effectively. Studies have shown that switching between tasks can decrease productivity by up to 40%. The brain requires time to adjust when moving from one activity to another, leading to cognitive overload and reduced efficiency. Time blocking combats this by encouraging deep work— sustained periods of focus on a single task— proven to enhance performance and creativity.

Structured time also profoundly impacts reducing decision fatigue. Every day, we make countless decisions, from the trivial to the significant, and each depletes our mental energy. By preplanning our tasks through time blocking, we eliminate the need to constantly decide what to do next, freeing up cognitive resources for more important decisions and creative thinking.

In a professional context, time blocking can dramatically improve productivity by ensuring that key projects receive the attention they deserve. It allows individuals and teams to set aside uninterrupted time for strategic work, leading to higher-quality outcomes and greater innovation. In personal life, time blocking can help balance work and leisure, ensuring that time is dedicated to self-care, hobbies, and relationships, leading to a more fulfilling life.

The benefits of time blocking extend beyond just getting more done. It fosters a sense of accomplishment and control, reducing stress and burnout. When we see our tasks completed within their designated time blocks, we gain confidence in our ability to manage our responsibilities and achieve our goals. Moreover, the structured approach of time blocking helps to build discipline, a critical factor in sustaining long-term success in any endeavor.

Time blocking is not merely a tool but a transformative practice that can elevate your productivity, enhance your well-being, and help you achieve a harmonious balance between work and life. Whether you are a professional striving for career success, a student managing academic demands, or an individual seeking more time for personal growth, time blocking offers a clear and effective path to unlocking your full potential.

Why Time Blocking Works:

Time blocking is not just a productivity hack but a method grounded in psychological principles that address some of the most common challenges we face in managing our time and energy. The effectiveness of time blocking lies in its ability to harness our natural cognitive tendencies while mitigating the pitfalls of modern work environments.

One of the key reasons time blocking works so well is its ability to reduce decision fatigue. Every day, we are faced with a multitude of choices, from the mundane to the critical. Each decision we make depletes our cognitive resources, leading to a state known as decision fatigue. This phenomenon can result in poor choices, procrastination, and a general decline in productivity. Time blocking preempts this by constantly eliminating the need to decide what to do next. By having a predetermined schedule, you conserve mental energy, allowing you to focus on executing tasks rather than determining which task to tackle.

In addition to reducing decision fatigue, time blocking significantly enhances focus. The modern work environment is rife with distractions, from constant email notifications to the lure of social media. Our brains are not designed to manage these incessant interruptions; we lose valuable time and momentum whenever we switch our attention from one task to another. Time blocking creates a structured environment where you can dedicate uninterrupted blocks of time to specific tasks. This practice is aligned with the concept of "deep work," where you engage in sustained, distraction-free focus, leading to higher-quality output and increased efficiency.

Furthermore, time blocking fosters a balanced life by ensuring that all areas of your life receive the attention they deserve. It is easy to let work consume all available time, leaving little room for personal pursuits, relaxation, or family. You create a more holistic schedule that promotes overall well-being by consciously allocating time blocks to various aspects of your life— such as work, exercise, hobbies, and social activities. This balance is essential for preventing burnout and maintaining long-term productivity and happiness.

Time blocking also taps into the psychological satisfaction of crossing tasks off a list. When you see your day unfold as planned, with tasks completed within their allocated time blocks, it provides a sense of accomplishment and progress. This positive reinforcement encourages you to continue using the technique, reinforcing a cycle of productivity and satisfaction.

Moreover, the discipline instilled by time blocking extends beyond completing tasks; it shapes how you approach your entire day. Knowing that you have dedicated time for specific activities allows you to be fully present in each moment, whether you are working on a complex project, enjoying a meal, or spending time with loved ones. This presence improves the quality of your work and enhances your individual experiences, leading to a more fulfilled life.

Time blocking works because it aligns with the way our minds function best. It reduces the cognitive load of decision-making, enhances our ability to focus, and maintains a balanced approach to life. By implementing time blocking, you can transform your productivity, reduce stress, and create a more intentional and satisfying daily routine.

What to Expect from This Book:

This book is your comprehensive guide to mastering the art of time blocking, a powerful technique that can dramatically enhance your productivity and overall well-being. Whether new to time blocking or looking to refine your existing approach, this book will provide the strategies, tools, and real-life examples necessary to make time blocking an integral part of your daily routine.

You can expect to explore various time-blocking strategies tailored to diverse needs and lifestyles. From basic setups for beginners to advanced techniques for those who want to optimize every minute of their day, the book will guide you through creating a system that works for you. We will delve into the psychology behind time blocking, helping you understand how to implement it and why it works so effectively.

The book is structured to take you from the foundational concepts of time blocking to the finer application details. We will start with an introduction to the principles of time blocking, ensuring you grasp the core ideas before moving on to more specific strategies. Whether you prefer a digital tool, a physical planner, or a hybrid approach, you will learn to set up your time-blocking system. We will also cover tailoring your time blocks to accommodate diverse tasks, from deep work sessions to routine maintenance activities.

Throughout the book, you will find practical tools and templates to assist you in implementing time blocking into your life. These resources are designed to make the process as seamless as possible, allowing you to quickly adapt and adapt time blocking to fit your unique circumstances. Whether it is templates for weekly planning, tips for overcoming common obstacles, or checklists to track your progress, these tools will support you in building a sustainable time-blocking practice.

Real-life examples will be woven throughout the book to illustrate how time blocking has been successfully used by individuals across different fields and stages of life. These stories will show you the versatility of time blocking, demonstrating how it can be applied in personal and professional contexts. You will read about entrepreneurs who use time blocking to juggle multiple business ventures, parents who balance work and family, and students who manage their academic workload more effectively. These examples will inspire you and provide practical insights into how time blocking can be customized to meet your goals.

In addition to strategies and examples, the book will address the challenges you may encounter. Time blocking is a flexible tool that requires discipline and adaptability, like any productivity system. We will discuss common pitfalls, such as over-scheduling, and offer solutions to help you stay on track. You will also learn how to adjust your time-blocking system as your priorities shift and your life evolves, ensuring it remains a valuable asset in your productivity toolkit.

By the end of this book, you will have a deep understanding of time blocking and how it can be leveraged to achieve your personal and professional aspirations. You will walk away with a customized time-blocking system ready to implement immediately and confidently maintained in the long term. This book is more than just a guide; it is a journey towards reclaiming your time, enhancing your focus, and living a more balanced and fulfilling life.

Chapter 1:
Understanding Time Blocking

What is Time Blocking?

Time blocking is a powerful and methodical approach to managing your time that allows you to plan your day in a way that prioritizes focus and productivity. Time blocking involves dividing your day into blocks dedicated to a specific task or related activities. Unlike more traditional time management techniques that rely on to-do lists or task prioritization, time blocking forces you to allocate specific time slots to your tasks, thus turning your schedule into a series of appointments with yourself.

The origins of time blocking can be traced back to some of history's most productive figures, including Benjamin Franklin and Leonardo da Vinci, who were known for their rigorous self-discipline in managing time. However, the concept became more formally recognized and structured with the advent of modern productivity theories. The practice was notably popularized in recent years by thought leaders in the productivity space, who have emphasized its effectiveness in combating the distractions and interruptions that characterize our fast-paced, digital world.

One key aspect differentiating time blocking from other time management techniques is its emphasis on intentionality. While to-do lists and the Pomodoro Technique help manage tasks, they often fall short in promoting deep focus and structured work. Time blocking, on the other hand, goes beyond just listing tasks; it involves scheduling when those tasks will be done, thereby creating a more organized and deliberate approach to your day. This technique acknowledges that time is a finite resource, and by pre-allocating it, you ensure that your most important tasks receive the attention they deserve.

Moreover, time blocking is inherently flexible, allowing for adjustments as needed. If unexpected tasks arise or a particular task requires more time than originally planned, you can shift your time blocks accordingly. This adaptability makes time blocking a practical tool for managing predictable and unpredictable schedule elements.

Another significant distinction of time blocking is its impact on reducing decision fatigue. Traditional time management often leaves individuals with tasks without clear guidance on when to tackle each. This lack of structure can lead to a constant need to decide what to do next, which can drain mental energy throughout the day. Time blocking removes this burden by providing a clear plan, reducing the number of decisions you must make, and allowing you to channel your energy into the tasks.

Time blocking also contrasts with techniques like multitasking, which often results in divided attention and lower-quality work. By focusing on one task per time block, you can engage in deep work, a peak concentration that enables you to produce your best work. This single-task focus is one of the reasons time blocking is particularly effective for projects that require creativity, problem-solving, or critical thinking.

Time blocking is more than just a time management technique; it is a comprehensive approach to structuring your day with purpose and clarity. By dedicating specific blocks of time to your tasks, you create a disciplined environment where focus and productivity can thrive. Its origins in the practices of history's most effective individuals, combined with its modern application, make time blocking a timeless and versatile tool for anyone looking to enhance their productivity and achieve their goals.

The Components of Time Blocking:

Understanding its core components is essential to effectively implementing time blocking. These elements work together to create a structured, balanced, and flexible schedule that maximizes productivity while allowing for the inevitable changes throughout the day. The key components of time blocking include blocks of time, tasks, priorities, and buffers.

Blocks of Time

The foundation of time blocking lies in the concept of blocks of time. These are designated periods within your day that are set aside for specific tasks or activities. Instead of letting your day be dictated by interruptions or an endless list of tasks, you assign specific time slots to your most important work. This structured approach ensures that each task has dedicated time, reducing the temptation to multitask and improving focus.

Blocks of time can vary in length depending on the nature of the task. For instance, deep work that requires intense concentration, such as writing or problem-solving, might be assigned longer blocks of 60 to 90 minutes. On the other hand, routine tasks or quick meetings only require shorter blocks of 15 to 30 minutes. The flexibility to adjust the length of your time blocks is one of the strengths of this technique, allowing you to tailor your schedule to the demands of your day.

Tasks

Tasks are the activities or responsibilities that fill your blocks of time. In time blocking, it is crucial to define your tasks before scheduling them. This clarity allows you to allocate appropriate time blocks to each task based on its complexity and priority. Tasks can range from professional duties, like project work or meetings, to personal commitments, such as exercise or family time.

When assigning tasks to time blocks, it is important to be realistic about how long each task will take. Overestimating or underestimating the time required can lead to frustration and disrupt the flow of your day. By gauging the time needed for each task, you ensure your schedule is manageable and effective.

Priorities

Prioritization is a critical component of time blocking. Not all tasks are created equally, and some will have a greater impact on your goals and success than others. Time blocking encourages you to identify and prioritize your most important tasks (MITs) before assigning them to your schedule. By doing so, you ensure that your most critical work is completed first, during the times when you are most alert and focused.

Priorities can be determined based on deadlines, the task's significance to your objectives, or energy levels. For example, you might prioritize tasks that require deep thinking during your peak productivity hours and reserve more routine or administrative tasks for periods when your energy naturally dips.

Buffers

Buffers are the unsung heroes of a well-constructed time-blocking schedule. These are small, flexible periods between your time blocks to account for the unexpected— overruns, interruptions, or unplanned tasks. Buffers help prevent your schedule from becoming too rigid and allow you to adapt to changes without derailing your entire day.

For example, if you have back-to-back meetings scheduled, a buffer between them can provide you with a few minutes to regroup, prepare for the next meeting, or oversee any urgent matters that arise. Buffers also offer breathing space, reducing the stress of feeling rushed or overwhelmed.

Incorporating buffers into your time-blocking schedule is an initiative-taking way to manage the unpredictability of daily life. While they may seem like minor additions, these small gaps can significantly enhance the flexibility and sustainability of your time-blocking system.

Together, blocks of time, tasks, priorities, and buffers form the backbone of an effective time-blocking strategy. Each component is crucial in creating a schedule that promotes productivity and maintains balance and adaptability. By understanding and integrating these elements into your daily routine, you can harness the full potential of time blocking, making it a powerful tool for managing your time, achieving your goals, and leading a more organized and fulfilling life.

Common Misconceptions:

While time blocking has proven to be an effective method for enhancing productivity and managing time, it is not without its share of misconceptions. These misunderstandings can sometimes deter people from blocking time or lead to frustration when they don't see immediate success. Addressing these common myths can help clarify what time blocking entails and how it can be adapted to suit various needs and work styles.

Myth 1: Time Blocking Is Too Rigid

One of the most prevalent misconceptions about time blocking is that it is overly rigid, leaving no room for flexibility or spontaneity. Critics often argue that time blocking creates a tightly packed schedule that can be easily disrupted by unforeseen events or changes in priorities. However, there is a misunderstanding of how time blocking can and should be implemented.

In reality, time blocking is a flexible tool that can be adapted to the dynamic nature of daily life. A well-constructed time-blocking schedule includes buffers— those small gaps between tasks that allow for adjustments, overruns, and unplanned activities. These buffers ensure that your day isn't derailed by the unexpected. Moreover, time blocking encourages regular review and adjustment of your schedule, making it a living document that evolves with your needs. Far from being rigid, time blocking is about creating a structure that supports flexibility, not stifles it.

Myth 2: Time Blocking Is Only for Specific Types of Work

Another common myth is that time blocking is only suitable for certain types of work, such as project-based tasks or creative endeavors, and does not apply to more routine or administrative duties. Some believe that time blocking is best suited for individuals in roles that require deep focus and long stretches of uninterrupted time, like writers or developers, and not for those with jobs that involve multitasking or frequent interruptions.

Time blocking is a versatile tool that can be applied to virtually any type of work. Whether managing complex projects, handling administrative tasks, or juggling multiple responsibilities, time blocking can help you create a balanced schedule. For example, routine tasks like answering emails or attending meetings can be time-blocked as effectively as more intensive work. By allocating specific times for these activities, you can manage them more efficiently, ensuring they don't consume your entire day. The nature of the work does not limit time blocking but rather enhances it by providing a clear framework within which all tasks, no matter how varied, can be managed.

Myth 3: Time Blocking Takes Too Much Time to Set Up

Some people avoid time blocking because they believe the initial setup is too time-consuming. Breaking down tasks, estimating the time required, and scheduling them into blocks might seem overwhelming, especially for those new to the practice. However, this initial investment of time is relatively small compared to the long-term benefits.

The reality is that time blocking requires some upfront effort, but this investment pays off in spades. Once you establish a routine, the process becomes more intuitive and less time-intensive. Moreover, the time spent setting up your blocks is often recouped through increased productivity and reduced stress. With practice, you'll find that creating your time-blocked schedule becomes a natural part of your daily or weekly planning, taking only a few minutes to complete.

Myth 4: Time Blocking Is Too Restrictive for Creative Work

There is a common belief that creativity cannot thrive under the constraints of a schedule and that time blocking is too restrictive for creative professionals. Some argue that creativity requires freedom and spontaneity, not the confines of a time-blocked day.

However, many creative professionals have found that time blocking enhances creativity by providing dedicated time for deep, uninterrupted work. Instead of stifling creativity, time blocking protects it by minimizing distractions during crucial periods of creative flow. You create an environment where creativity can flourish by scheduling time for brainstorming, drafting, or other creative processes. The structure provided by time blocking can also help manage the more routine aspects of creative work, such as editing or administrative tasks, freeing up more mental space for innovative thinking.

Myth 5: Time Blocking Is Only for Highly Disciplined People

Finally, there is a misconception that time blocking is only effective for those naturally disciplined or highly organized. This belief can discourage individuals who struggle with procrastination or disorganization from attempting time blocking.

In truth, time blocking is a tool that can help cultivate discipline, not just a method for those who already possess it. By breaking the day into manageable chunks, time blocking provides a clear roadmap, making it easier to stay on track. It helps build momentum by creating a sense of accomplishment as each time block is completed. Over time, this practice can foster greater self-discipline and improve overall time management skills, even for those who initially find it challenging.

Time blocking is a powerful and adaptable time management technique, but like any tool, it is subject to misconceptions. By understanding its flexibility, versatility, and accessibility, you can approach it with the right mindset and avoid the pitfalls of these common myths. Whether you're looking to boost productivity, manage a diverse workload, or create more balance in your life, time blocking offers a practical solution that can be tailored to your unique needs and goals.

Chapter 2:
Getting Started with Time Blocking

Assessing Your Current Schedule:

Before you can effectively implement time blocking, it is essential to gain a clear understanding of how you currently spend your time. Assessing your existing schedule is the first step in this process, allowing you to identify patterns, inefficiencies, and opportunities for improvement. By analyzing your daily routines, you can uncover where your time is going, which tasks consume the most energy, and where adjustments can be made to optimize your productivity.

Assessing your current schedule begins with a simple but revealing exercise: time tracking. For one week, document how you spend every hour of your day. This includes work-related tasks, personal activities, leisure, and even downtime. It's important to be as detailed as possible, noting the tasks and the transitions between them. For example, include these details if you spent 15 minutes checking emails between meetings or took a short break to browse social media.

Once you have a week's worth of data, it's time to analyze it. Begin by categorizing your activities into different groups, such as work, personal care, leisure, errands, and unplanned interruptions. This categorization will help you see how much time is devoted to each area of your life. You may find, for instance, that a significant portion of your day is spent on low-value tasks or that unplanned interruptions are taking more time than you realized.

Next, identify the tasks that take up the most time. Are these tasks aligned with your priorities and goals? If not, they might be delegation, automation, or elimination candidates. For example, if you notice that you're spending much time on administrative work that could be streamlined, time blocking can help you create more efficiency in this area.

It is also important to look at the flow of your day. Are there natural peaks and troughs in your energy levels? Do certain activities consistently take longer than expected? This information is crucial when it comes to setting up your time blocks. For instance, if you have the most energy in the morning, this might be the ideal time to schedule your most important or challenging tasks.

Additionally, consider the transitions between tasks. If you notice that you're losing time switching from one activity to another, this might indicate a need for better task batching or fewer interruptions. Time blocking can help reduce these inefficiencies by grouping similar tasks and setting aside specific transition times.

Another key assessment aspect is how much time you dedicate to planning versus doing. While planning is essential, it's easy to fall into the trap of over-planning, which can reduce the time available for actual work. If planning or meetings take up too much of your day, time blocking can help you allocate enough time for these activities without letting them dominate your schedule.

Finally, reflect on your personal and leisure time. Are you getting enough rest, exercise, and relaxation? If not, this is a sign that your current schedule may be too work-focused, leaving little room for self-care and personal growth. Time blocking isn't just about work; it's about creating a balanced life. By assessing your current schedule, you can ensure that time is set aside for the things that truly matter to you, both professionally and personally.

Assessing your current schedule is an eye-opening process that lays the groundwork for successful time blocking. It provides a clear picture of how you're currently managing your time and highlights areas where changes are needed. With this knowledge, you can confidently move forward, ready to design a time-blocking system that aligns with your goals, maximizes your productivity, and enhances your overall well-being.

Setting Clear Goals:

Once you've assessed your current schedule, setting clear goals is the next step in implementing time blocking. Defining what you want to achieve through time blocking is crucial, as it provides direction and purpose to your efforts. These goals will guide how you structure your time blocks, helping you stay focused and motivated as you work towards both short-term milestones and long-term aspirations.

Short-Term Goals: Building Momentum and Establishing Habits

Short-term goals are those you aim to achieve within a relatively short period, such as days, weeks, or months. In time blocking, these goals often revolve around improving immediate productivity, managing specific projects, or developing new habits.

Start by identifying the areas of your life or work that need immediate attention. Perhaps you're struggling to keep up with deadlines, finding it hard to focus during work hours, or feeling overwhelmed by your to-do list. Your short-term goals might include completing a particular project, reducing time spent on distractions, or creating a more balanced daily routine.

For example, if your current schedule shows you're spending too much time on low-priority tasks, a short-term goal might be reallocating that time toward more impactful activities. Or, if you consistently feel stressed by the end of the day, a short-term goal could be to incorporate regular breaks into your schedule to recharge and maintain energy levels.

As you define these goals, be specific. Instead of setting a vague goal like "be more productive," aim for something measurable, such as "reduce time spent on email by 30% over the next two weeks." Clear, specific goals give you a concrete target to aim for, making it easier to track your progress and adjust as needed.

Long-Term Goals: Creating Sustainable Success

While short-term goals help you address immediate challenges, long-term goals focus on where you want to be. These goals are about creating lasting change and achieving significant milestones in your personal and professional life. Time blocking is not just a tool for getting through the day; it's a strategy for building the life you want over the long term.

Your long-term goals may include advancing your career, achieving a work-life balance that allows for personal fulfillment, or mastering a new skill. These goals often require sustained effort and consistent focus, where time-blocking shines.

For instance, if your long-term goal is to write a book, time blocking can help you allocate regular writing sessions that build up over time, turning a daunting project into manageable tasks. Similarly, suppose you want to achieve a better work-life balance. In that case, you might set long-term goals around reducing overtime, increasing quality family time, or dedicating more time to hobbies and self-care.

As with short-term goals, specificity is key. Define what success looks like for you in the long term. Instead of simply saying, "I want to be more successful," outline what success means— reaching a certain position in your career, earning a specific income, or achieving a personal milestone like completing a marathon or learning a new language.

Aligning Short-Term and Long-Term Goals

A crucial aspect of goal-setting in time blocking is ensuring that your short-term efforts align with your long-term aspirations. This alignment ensures that the time you invest daily contributes to your broader vision for the future. When setting short-term goals, consider how they fit into your long-term plans. Each task you time block should move you closer to your ultimate objectives.

For example, if your long-term goal is to improve your health, your short-term goals include scheduling regular workouts, meal planning, or learning about nutrition. Over time, these consistent actions will accumulate, leading to significant health improvements.

Review and Adjust

Goal setting is not a one-time activity. As you progress, regularly review your goals and adjust them as necessary. Life is dynamic, and your priorities may shift over time. By periodically reassessing your goals, you can ensure that your time blocking remains relevant and effective.

Setting clear goals is the foundation of successful time blocking. By defining what you want to achieve in the short and long term, you create a roadmap that guides your daily actions and ensures your time is spent on what truly matters. Whether you aim to boost productivity, achieve a major milestone, or create a more balanced life, time blocking with well-defined goals can help you turn your ambitions into reality.

Identifying Priorities:

Identifying your priorities is critical in time blocking to ensure your schedule aligns with your goals and values. With so many demands on our time, it can be challenging to determine what truly deserves our attention. Fortunately, several techniques can help you clarify your priorities, making it easier to allocate your time blocks effectively. One of the most powerful tools for this purpose is the Eisenhower Matrix.

The Eisenhower Matrix: A Tool for Prioritization

The Eisenhower Matrix, also known as the Urgent-Important Matrix, is a simple yet effective tool for categorizing tasks based on their urgency and importance. Named after President Dwight D. Eisenhower, who famously used this method to prioritize his decisions, the matrix divides tasks into four quadrants:

1. **Urgent and Important:** Tasks that require immediate attention and have significant consequences if not completed. These are often crises, deadlines, or pressing problems that must be addressed promptly.

2. **Important but Not Urgent:** Tasks crucial for long-term success don't need to be done immediately. These include strategic planning, relationship building, and personal development

activities. While they can be postponed, doing so repeatedly can lead to missed opportunities and long-term setbacks.

3. **Urgent but Not Important:** Tasks that demand immediate attention but don't significantly contribute to your long-term goals. These are often interruptions, requests from others, or minor issues that could be delegated or minimized.

4. **Not Urgent and Not Important:** Tasks that are neither pressing nor valuable in the grand scheme of things. These include time-wasting activities and distractions that do little to advance your goals.

To use the Eisenhower Matrix, list all the tasks and activities you must manage. Then, categorize each one into one of the four quadrants. This exercise will give you a clear visual representation of where your time is currently going and which tasks deserve the most attention.

Prioritizing Tasks Based on the Eisenhower Matrix

Once you've categorized your tasks, the next step is to prioritize them within your time-blocking schedule:

- ➢ **Focus on the Important and Not Urgent Quadrant:** This is where time blocking can have the most profound impact. By allocating dedicated time blocks to these tasks, you ensure that important but often neglected activities, such as strategic planning or personal growth, receive the attention they deserve. These tasks are the key to long-term success and fulfillment.

- ➢ **Manage Urgent and Important Tasks Efficiently:** These tasks should be addressed promptly. However, effectively managing the Important but Not Urgent tasks can reduce the number of crises in this category. Time blocking can help you allocate specific periods for these tasks, ensuring they don't overwhelm your schedule.

- ➢ **Delegate or Minimize Urgent but Not Important Tasks:** Where possible, delegate these tasks to others or find ways to minimize their impact on your day. If you can't delegate, limit your time on these activities by setting strict time blocks.

- **Eliminate or Avoid Not Urgent and Not Important Tasks**: These tasks are often distractions that can be eliminated or avoided altogether. Time blocking can help by making you more aware of how you spend your time and allowing you to choose activities that align with your priorities consciously.

Other Techniques for Identifying Priorities

In addition to the Eisenhower Matrix, there are other techniques you can use to identify and prioritize your tasks:

- **Pareto Principle (80/20 Rule)**: This principle suggests that 80% of your results come from 20% of your efforts. By identifying and focusing on the tasks that fall into this 20%, you can maximize your productivity and ensure your time is spent on activities with the greatest impact.

- **ABC Method**: This method categorizes tasks as A, B, or C based on importance. "A" tasks are the most critical, "B" tasks are important but less so, and "C" tasks are nice-to-do but not essential. This method helps you quickly assess which tasks should take priority.

- **MoSCoW Method**: Project management often uses this technique to prioritize features or tasks. It categorizes tasks as Must have, Should have, Could have, or Won't have. This method can help you determine which tasks are non-negotiable and which can be postponed or dropped.

Aligning Priorities with Goals

Identifying priorities is not just about managing tasks; it is about aligning your actions with your goals and values. As you use these techniques to determine your priorities, always keep your short-term and long-term goals in mind. This alignment ensures that your time blocks are not just filled with tasks but are strategically designed to move you closer to your desired outcomes.

Identifying your priorities is a crucial step in time blocking. Tools like the Eisenhower Matrix and other prioritization techniques ensure that your time is spent on activities that matter most, leading to greater productivity, satisfaction, and success.

Chapter 3:
Designing Your Time Blocks

Creating Effective Time Blocks:

Designing your time blocks is where the planning meets action in the time-blocking process. It's about transforming your goals and priorities into a structured, practical schedule that guides your daily activities. Effective time blocks reflect what you must accomplish and when and how to best achieve those tasks. Here is a step-by-step guide to creating time blocks that align with your goals and priorities.

Step 1: Start with Your Goals and Priorities

Before designing your time blocks, revisit the goals and priorities you have already established. Whether short-term or long-term, your time blocks should be directly linked to these objectives. Ask yourself, "What tasks are most important to achieving my goals?" and "What activities need to be prioritized in my schedule?" These questions will help you identify the tasks that need to be allocated time first.

Step 2: Determine Your Peak Productivity Times

Everyone has certain times of the day when they are naturally more focused and energetic. For some, this might be early in the morning; for others, it could be later in the afternoon. Identifying your peak productivity times allows you to schedule your most demanding tasks when you're at your best. This alignment between your energy levels and task difficulty can significantly boost your efficiency and the quality of your work.

To determine your peak times, reflect on your daily rhythms or even track your energy levels over a week. Once identified, block out these times for your most critical or challenging tasks.

Step 3: Categorize Your Tasks

Next, categorize your tasks based on their nature and the type of focus they require. Tasks can be divided into categories such as deep work (tasks that require intense concentration), routine work (tasks that are necessary but don't require much mental effort), and personal activities (such as exercise or relaxation).

Deep work tasks should be scheduled during peak productivity times, while routine tasks can be allocated to periods when your energy naturally dips. Personal activities should be interspersed throughout the day to provide balance and prevent burnout.

Step 4: Allocate Specific Time Blocks

With your tasks categorized and your peak times identified, it is time to allocate specific blocks of time to each task. The length of each time block should correspond to the nature of the task and your ability to maintain focus. For instance, deep work might require longer time blocks of 60 to 90 minutes, while routine tasks could be handled in shorter 15 to 30-minute blocks.

Be realistic about how long each task will take, and avoid overloading your schedule. It's better to allocate more time than you think you'll need, especially when starting with time blocking. This will help you avoid frustration and allow you to adjust as needed.

Step 5: Include Buffers and Breaks

Effective time blocks are not just about work; they also include time for breaks and buffers. Buffers are short periods between tasks that account for overruns, transitions, or unexpected interruptions. These are essential for maintaining the flow of your day and preventing your schedule from becoming too rigid.

Breaks are equally important, allowing you to rest and recharge between tasks. Consider using techniques like the Pomodoro method, where you work for a set period (e.g., 25 minutes) and then take a short break (e.g., 5 minutes). Incorporating regular breaks into your schedule helps sustain productivity and prevents burnout.

Step 6: Review and Adjust

Once you have created your time blocks, put them into practice and see how they work for you. Time blocking is an iterative process, meaning you should regularly review your schedule and adjust based on what is working and what is not. If you find certain tasks are taking longer than expected, adjust your time blocks accordingly. If your energy levels dip at certain times, consider shifting tasks to align with your natural rhythms better.

Regular review and adjustment ensure that your time blocking remains a dynamic tool that evolves with your needs, helping you stay on track with your goals and maintain balance in your life.

Step 7: Commit to the Process

Creating effective time blocks is only part of the equation; committing to following them is the real key. This means treating your time blocks as non-negotiable appointments with yourself. While flexibility is important, and you should adapt as necessary, maintaining discipline in sticking to your time blocks will yield the best results over time.

Following these steps, you can create time blocks that reflect your goals and priorities and fit seamlessly into your daily life. Whether working towards a major project or simply trying to manage your day-to-day tasks more efficiently, well-designed time blocks can be powerful in achieving your objectives and maintaining a balanced, productive life.

Finding the Right Duration: How to Determine the Optimal Length of Time for Different Tasks, Balancing Focus and Productivity

One key factor in successful time blocking is finding the right duration for each task. The length of your time blocks can significantly impact your ability to maintain focus, manage your energy, and ultimately enhance your productivity. Different tasks require different amounts of time, and understanding how to allocate these time blocks effectively is essential for maximizing efficiency.

Understanding Task Complexity and Focus Requirements

The first step in determining the right duration for your time blocks is to assess each task's complexity and focus requirements. Tasks that require deep concentration, such as writing, problem-solving, or strategic planning, generally benefit from longer time blocks. These are often called "deep work" tasks, where you need uninterrupted time to dive deep into the work and produce high-quality results.

On the other hand, routine tasks, such as answering emails, administrative work, or scheduling, typically require less focus and can be completed in shorter bursts. While necessary, these tasks don't require the same cognitive effort and can often be batched together in smaller time blocks.

Balancing Focus and Breaks

To maintain peak productivity, it's important to balance focus and breaks. Research has shown that the human brain can only maintain high levels of focus for a limited time before it begins to fatigue. The optimal duration for deep work tasks typically ranges between 60 and 90 minutes. Beyond this point, your ability to concentrate diminishes, and the quality of your work may suffer.

After a deep work session, taking a short break, typically around 5 to 15 minutes, is beneficial to recharge before moving on to the next task. These breaks help refresh your mind, reduce mental fatigue, and prepare you for the next period of focused work. Techniques like the Pomodoro method, which involves working for 25 minutes followed by a 5-minute break, are popular for managing shorter tasks or maintaining sustained focus over longer periods.

Tailoring Duration to Your Energy Levels

Everyone has different energy patterns throughout the day, often called "chronotypes." Some people are most productive in the morning, while others hit their stride later in the afternoon or evening. Understanding your energy levels can help you tailor the duration of your time blocks to match when you are at your best.

For example, if you are a morning person, you might schedule your longest and most demanding time blocks during the early hours, when your energy and focus peak. Conversely, suppose you find your energy waning in the afternoon. In that case, you might opt for shorter, less demanding time blocks during this period, reserving more challenging tasks for when you're naturally more alert.

Adjusting for Task Variety

Not all tasks are created equal, and even within the same category of work, different tasks might require varying amounts of time. It is important to be flexible and adjust the duration of your time blocks based on the specific nature of the task. For instance, a brainstorming session might only need 30 minutes, while drafting a report could require a full 90-minute block.

When determining the duration, consider factors like the estimated complexity of the task, any previous experience with similar tasks, and how mentally taxing the work is. It's also helpful to build a small buffer at the end of each time block to accommodate any unexpected overruns, ensuring you don't fall behind schedule.

Experimenting and Refining

Finding the right duration for your time blocks is often a process of experimentation and refinement. Start with a general guideline— for example, 60 minutes for deep work and 30 minutes for routine tasks— and then adjust based on your experiences. Pay attention to how you feel during and after each time block. Are you consistently running out of time, or do you lose focus before the block ends? Use these observations to fine-tune your schedule.

Over time, you will better understand the optimal durations for different types of tasks, allowing you to create a more effective and personalized time-blocking system.

Finding the right duration for your time blocks is essential for balancing focus and productivity. By considering your tasks' complexity and focus requirements, tailoring your schedule to your energy levels, and being willing to experiment and adjust, you can design time blocks that help you work more efficiently and effectively. Whether tackling deep work or routine tasks, the right time block duration can make all the difference in achieving your goals and maintaining a balanced, productive day.

Using Buffers and Breaks:

When designing an effective time-blocking schedule, incorporating buffers and breaks is essential for sustaining energy, focus, and overall productivity. These elements provide necessary downtime and offer flexibility, ensuring your schedule remains manageable and adaptable to the unexpected.

The Role of Buffers in Time-Blocking

Buffers are short periods inserted between your scheduled time blocks. These buffers provide a cushion, allowing for transitions between tasks, handling unexpected interruptions, or accommodating functions that take longer than anticipated. Without buffers, your schedule can become too rigid, leading to stress and frustration when things don't go as planned.

Why Buffers Are Important:

1. **Transition Time**: Moving from one task to another requires a mental shift, especially if the functions differ significantly. Buffers give you the time to reset and refocus before diving into the next activity. For example, after finishing a deep work session, a buffer allows you to mentally switch gears before starting a meeting or tackling routine tasks.

2. **Handling Overruns**: It is common for tasks to take longer than expected. Buffers act as a safety net, preventing your entire schedule from being thrown off if one task overruns its allotted time. This flexibility helps you stay on track without feeling rushed or stressed.

3. **Accommodating the Unexpected**: Life is unpredictable, and unexpected events or tasks can arise at any time. Buffers allow

you to address these unplanned activities without derailing your entire day.

How to Use Buffers Effectively:

- ➤ **Duration:** A typical buffer might be 5 to 15 minutes, depending on the nature of your tasks and your needed transition time. For more complex transitions, you might opt for a longer buffer.

- ➤ **Placement:** Place buffers between tasks that require different levels of focus or energy or after particularly intense work sessions to give yourself a moment to decompress. They can also be scheduled before and after meetings to account for preparation and follow-up.

- ➤ **Flexibility:** View buffers as flexible time slots that can be adjusted or repurposed. If you don't need the full buffer for a particular transition, you can use the remaining time for a quick break or a head start on your next task.

The Importance of Regular Breaks

While buffers provide short periods of flexibility between tasks, regular breaks are essential for maintaining long-term focus and energy throughout your day. Breaks allow your mind and body to rest, reducing the risk of burnout and helping you sustain productivity over extended periods.

Why Breaks Are Important:

1. **Mental Rest:** Continuous work without breaks can lead to cognitive fatigue, making it harder to focus and think clearly. Breaks allow your brain to recover, improving concentration and decision-making when you return to work.

2. **Physical Health:** Sitting or working in one position for too long can lead to physical discomfort or strain. Regular breaks encourage you to move around, stretch, and avoid the physical downsides of prolonged sedentary activity.

3. **Creativity and Problem-Solving**: Stepping away from a task, even for a short break, can enhance creativity and problem-solving. Breaks provide the mental space for ideas to incubate and for new perspectives to emerge.

How to Schedule Breaks Effectively:

- **Short Breaks**: Incorporate short breaks of 5 to 10 minutes after every 25 to 30 minutes of focused work. This approach, similar to the Pomodoro Technique, helps maintain consistent productivity while preventing burnout.

- **Longer Breaks**: Include longer breaks of 15 to 30 minutes after completing 90 minutes to 2 hours of work. These breaks allow more substantial rest, allowing you to eat, walk, or engage in a different activity before returning to work.

- **Mindful Breaks**: Use breaks to engage in relaxing or energizing activities. Whether taking a walk, practicing mindfulness, or simply stepping away from your workspace, the key is doing something that genuinely refreshes you.

Integrating Buffers and Breaks into Your Schedule

To ensure your schedule remains productive and sustainable, incorporate buffers and breaks into your time blocks. For example, if you plan a deep work session from 9:00 to 10:30 AM, you might include a 10-minute buffer afterward, followed by a 15-minute break before moving on to your next task. This structure allows you to work efficiently while being flexible to handle unexpected needs.

By strategically using buffers and breaks, you can create a time-blocking schedule that maximizes productivity and supports your overall well-being. These elements are crucial for sustaining focus, energy, and creativity throughout your day, helping you achieve your goals without sacrificing health or peace of mind.

Chapter 4:
Tools and Techniques for Time Blocking

Digital Tools for Time Blocking:

Various apps and software tools in the digital age help you effectively implement and manage time blocking. These digital tools can simplify creating, adjusting, and tracking your time blocks, making it easier to stay organized and focused. Here's an overview of some of the most popular and versatile tools you can use for time blocking, including Google Calendar, Notion, and Trello.

Google Calendar

Google Calendar is one of the most widely used digital tools for scheduling and time management, making it an excellent choice for time blocking. Its user-friendly interface and seamless integration with other Google services make creating and managing your time blocks easy.

Key Features:

- ➤ **Drag-and-Drop Interface**: You can easily create time blocks by dragging and dropping events into your calendar. This feature makes it simple to adjust your schedule as needed.

- ➤ **Color-Coding**: Google Calendar allows you to color-code your events, helping you visually differentiate between types of tasks, such as work, personal, or leisure activities.

- ➤ **Notifications and Reminders**: Set reminders for your time blocks to ensure you stay on track. Google Calendar can send messages to your devices, helping you transition smoothly from one task to another.

- ➤ **Recurring Events**: For tasks that happen regularly, such as weekly meetings or daily exercise, you can create recurring time

- blocks, which will save you time in scheduling and ensure consistency.
- **Integration:** Google Calendar integrates well with other productivity tools and apps, such as Google Tasks and Google Keep, allowing you to manage your tasks and notes alongside your time blocks.

Notion

The notion is a highly customizable productivity tool that combines note-taking, task management, and databases into one platform. It's ideal for those who prefer a more flexible and personalized approach to time blocking.

Key Features:

- **Customizable Pages and Databases:** Notion allows you to create pages and databases tailored to your needs. For example, you can set up a time-blocking system with calendars, to-do lists, and trackers all in one place.
- **Templates:** Notion offers a wide range of time-blocking templates, including daily planners, weekly schedules, and project timelines. These templates can be easily customized to fit your workflow.
- **Linked Databases:** You can link databases within Notion, allowing you to track tasks, goals, and time blocks together. This feature is particularly useful for managing complex projects with multiple moving parts.
- **Integration with Other Tools:** Notion integrates with various apps and services, such as Google Drive, Trello, and Slack, enabling you to centralize your work and time management.
- **Flexibility:** Notion's flexibility is one of its greatest strengths. You can adapt it to suit your specific time-blocking method, whether you prefer a daily agenda, a Kanban board, or a weekly overview.

Trello

Trello is a popular project management tool that uses a visual, card-based system to help you organize tasks and projects. It is particularly well-suited for those who enjoy a more visual approach to time blocking.

Key Features:

- **Kanban-Style Boards:** Trello's Kanban boards allow you to create columns for different time blocks or types of tasks. You can move cards between columns as tasks progress, providing a clear visual representation of your schedule.
- **Card Details and Checklists:** Each Trello card can contain detailed information about the task, including due dates, checklists, attachments, and comments. This makes it easy to track progress and stay organized.
- **Labels and Tags:** Trello offers customizable labels and tags, allowing you to categorize tasks by priority, project, or type. This feature helps you quickly identify what needs to be done and when.
- **Integration with Other Apps:** Trello integrates with numerous other tools, such as Google Calendar, Slack, and Evernote, enabling you to sync your time blocks across different platforms.
- **Automation:** Trello offers automation features through its Butler tool. This tool can automate repetitive tasks, such as moving cards or assigning due dates, helping streamline your time-blocking process.

Choosing the Right Tool for You

The best digital tool for time blocking depends on your personal preferences and the complexity of your schedule. Google Calendar is perfect for those who need a straightforward, easy-to-use calendar system. The notion is ideal for users who require a highly customizable and integrated workspace, while Trello is great for visual thinkers who benefit from a card-based, Kanban-style system.

When selecting a tool, consider how it fits into your existing workflow and whether it offers the features you need to manage your time blocks effectively. Each tool can be adapted to suit various time-blocking styles, helping you stay organized, focused, and productive.

Analog Tools and Planners:

While digital tools offer convenience and flexibility, many people find that analog tools such as physical planners, notebooks, and whiteboards provide a more tangible and satisfying way to manage their time. The tactile experience of writing by hand and the visual impact of seeing your schedule in front of you can enhance focus, creativity, and commitment to your time blocks. Here's how you can effectively use analog tools for time blocking.

Physical Planners

Physical planners are a popular choice for those who appreciate the ritual of writing and the satisfaction of turning pages. They come in various formats, from daily and weekly planners to bullet journals, offering a range of options to suit different time management needs.

Key Benefits:

- **Tactile Engagement**: Writing by hand can help reinforce memory and commitment to your tasks. It also provides a break from screen time, which can be refreshing and reduce digital fatigue.

- **Personalization**: Many physical planners allow for a high degree of personalization. You can choose a layout that suits your needs- a simple daily agenda or a more complex system with sections for goals, priorities, and notes.

- **Mindful Planning**: Writing in a physical planner encourages a slower, more thoughtful approach to planning. This mindfulness can help you make more intentional decisions about allocating your time.

Using Physical Planners for Time Blocking:

- ➢ **Daily or Weekly Layouts:** Choose a planner with daily or weekly layouts that provide ample space for time blocking. Use the hour-by-hour sections to assign specific tasks to each time block, and use margins or blank spaces for notes and reflections.

- ➢ **Color-Coding:** To visually differentiate between types of tasks, use colored pens or highlighters. For example, you might use blue for work-related tasks, green for personal activities, and red for urgent priorities.

- ➢ **Stickers and Washi Tape:** Many planners offer stickers or washi tape to mark important dates, highlight priorities, or add a personal touch to your schedule. These visual cues can make your planner more engaging and easier to navigate.

Notebooks and Bullet Journals

For those who prefer a more flexible and creative approach, notebooks and bullet journals offer a blank canvas for time blocking. A bullet journal, in particular, allows you to design your layouts and track various aspects of your life in one place.

Key Benefits:

- ➢ **Customization:** You have complete control over the layout and design with a notebook or bullet journal. You can create spreads that combine time blocking with habit tracking, goal setting, and reflections.

- ➢ **Creativity:** Notebooks' open-ended nature encourages creativity. You can experiment with different layouts, incorporate doodles, and use calligraphy to make your time blocking more enjoyable and personalized.

- ➢ **All-in-One System:** A bullet journal can be an all-in-one system, combining your planner, to-do lists, and notes in a single place.

This integration can help streamline your time management process.

Using Notebooks and Bullet Journals for Time Blocking:

- ➢ **Design Your Layout:** Start by designing a layout that suits your needs. You might create a weekly spread with sections for each day's time blocks or a daily page with time blocks and space for notes and tasks.

- ➢ **Symbol System:** Bullet journals often use symbols (bullets, dots, arrows) to track the status of tasks. Incorporate a symbol system to identify completed tasks, rescheduled items, or priorities quickly.

- ➢ **Habit Trackers:** Consider adding habit trackers to your journal to monitor how well you're sticking to your time blocks and achieving your goals. This visual feedback can motivate and help you adjust your schedule as needed.

Whiteboards

Whiteboards are another excellent tool for those who prefer a highly visual and interactive approach to time blocking. They are particularly useful for people who like to see their entire schedule at a glance and make quick adjustments.

Key Benefits:

- ➢ **Visibility:** A whiteboard offers large, clear visibility of your schedule, making it easy to see what's coming up and where you have open time slots.

- ➢ **Flexibility:** The ability to quickly erase and rewrite on a whiteboard allows easy adjustments to your time blocks. This flexibility is ideal for those with dynamic schedules that require frequent changes.

- ➢ **Team Collaboration:** A whiteboard can be a shared scheduling tool if you work in a team or household. Everyone can see the plan for the day or week, making it easier to coordinate tasks and responsibilities.

Using Whiteboards for Time Blocking:

> - **Daily or Weekly View:** Create a daily or weekly view on your whiteboard, dividing the space into time blocks. Use different colored markers for different types of tasks or activities.
>
> - **Magnetic Accessories:** Consider using magnetic accessories, such as magnets or clipboards, to add more functionality to your whiteboard. These can hold notes, reminders, or important documents.
>
> - **Checklists and Goals:** Dedicate a section of your whiteboard to checklists or goals. As you complete tasks, check them off, giving you a visual sense of accomplishment.

Analog tools like physical planners, notebooks, and whiteboards offer a tactile, engaging way to manage your time through time blocking. Whether you prefer the structured layout of a planner, the creative freedom of a bullet journal, or the visual impact of a whiteboard, these tools can help you stay organized and focused. By choosing the right analog tool for your needs, you can create a time-blocking system that is both effective and personally satisfying.

Integrating Time Blocking with Other Productivity Systems:

Time blocking is a versatile productivity technique that can be effectively combined with other established systems to create a powerful, personalized approach to managing your time and tasks. By integrating time blocking with methods like the Pomodoro Technique, Getting Things Done (GTD), or Agile practices, you can enhance productivity, maintain focus, and achieve your goals more efficiently. Here is how you can merge these approaches to maximize your productivity.

The Pomodoro Technique

The Pomodoro Technique is a time management method that involves breaking work into intervals, typically 25 minutes long, followed by a short break. Each 25-minute session is called a "Pomodoro." After completing four Pomodoros, you take a longer break. This technique enhances focus and reduces mental fatigue by balancing work with regular rest periods.

Integrating Time Blocking with the Pomodoro Technique:

- ➢ **Set Time Blocks as Pomodoro Sessions:** Use time blocks that align with the Pomodoro intervals. For instance, if you have a time block dedicated to deep work, break it into multiple 25-minute Pomodoro sessions. This approach helps you maintain intense focus while ensuring you take regular breaks.

- ➢ **Plan Your Day Around Pomodoro:** Structure your time blocks around the Pomodoro intervals. For example, you might allocate two Pomodoro (50 minutes) for writing, followed by a 5-minute break, and then another two Pomodoro for a different task. This method allows you to maintain momentum throughout the day.

- ➢ **Track Progress Within Time Blocks:** Use a Pomodoro timer to track your progress within each time block. This tracking can help you stay committed to your tasks and provide a sense of accomplishment as you complete each Pomodoro.

Getting Things Done (GTD)

Getting Things Done (GTD) is a productivity system developed by David Allen that focuses on capturing tasks, clarifying what needs to be done, organizing tasks into actionable steps, reviewing progress, and engaging with tasks based on context, time, and energy levels.

Integrating Time Blocking with GTD:

- ➢ **Capture and Clarify Tasks:** Use GTD's capture and clarify steps to collect all your tasks and break them into actionable items. Once you have a clear list of tasks, use time blocking to schedule specific time slots for each action.

- ➢ **Organize by Context and Energy Levels:** GTD emphasizes organizing tasks based on context (where and what tools you have) and energy levels. When setting up your time blocks, consider the context and energy required for each task and allocate time accordingly. For example, schedule high-energy tasks like brainstorming in the morning and lower-energy tasks like email management in the afternoon.

- **Weekly Review with Time Blocking**: Use GTD's weekly review process to assess your progress and adjust your time blocks for the upcoming week. This review ensures that your schedule remains aligned with your goals and that all tasks are accounted for.

Agile Practices

Agile practices, commonly used in software development and project management, emphasize flexibility, collaboration, and iterative progress. Agile methodologies like Scrum involve working in short, focused sprints with regular check-ins and adjustments.

Integrating Time Blocking with Agile Practices:

- **Sprint Planning with Time Blocking**: Use time blocking to plan your sprints. Allocate specific blocks of time for different tasks or user stories within the sprint. This approach helps you ensure that all functions are covered and that you progress steadily toward your sprint goals.

- **Daily Stand-Ups and Time Blocks**: Integrate daily stand-up meetings into your time blocks. Dedicate a specific time block each morning for the stand-up, followed by blocks for completing the tasks discussed in the meeting. This structure keeps your day organized and aligned with the team's objectives.

- **Review and Retrospective Time Blocks**: At the end of each sprint, schedule time blocks for the review and retrospective sessions. These blocks allow you to reflect on what went well, identify areas for improvement, and plan the next sprint accordingly.

Combining Multiple Systems

You can also combine elements from multiple productivity systems to create a hybrid approach that suits your unique needs:

➢ **Pomodoro and GTD**: Use GTD to organize your tasks and the Pomodoro Technique within your time blocks to maintain focus and momentum. For example, during your time blocks for GTD's "Next Actions," break tasks into Pomodoros to ensure steady progress.

➢ **Agile and GTD**: Integrate GTD's weekly review into Agile's sprint planning to ensure that your sprints align with your broader goals and that no tasks are overlooked.

➢ **Time Blocking and Reflection**: Make sure to include time blocks for reflection and adjustment, no matter which systems you integrate. Regularly reviewing your progress and tweaking your approach ensures that your productivity system remains effective and adaptable.

Integrating time blocking with other productivity systems like the Pomodoro Technique, GTD, and Agile practices allows you to create a tailored approach that maximizes productivity. By combining these methods, you can benefit from the strengths of each system— whether it is maintaining focus, staying organized, or working flexibly within a team. The key is experimenting with different combinations and finding what works best for you, ensuring that your time-blocking system is effective and aligned with your goals.

Chapter 5:
Implementing Time Blocking in Daily Life

Morning Routines and Planning:

Starting your day with a structured morning routine sets the tone for a productive and focused day, and time blocking plays a crucial role in this process. When you begin your day with time blocking, you create a clear, intentional plan that guides you through your tasks and priorities, allowing you to maximize your productivity while maintaining flexibility.

The first step in implementing time blocking into your morning routine is to establish a consistent wake-up time. Consistency in waking up aligns your body's internal clock and provides a reliable foundation for your time blocks. Upon waking, dedicate a few minutes to a morning ritual that centers you— this could be as simple as deep breathing, meditation, or a quick stretch. This initial block of time is a mental transition from rest to readiness, preparing your mind for the day ahead.

Next, consider your primary goals for the day and use them to set up your morning blocks. This typically involves identifying your most critical tasks— those that require the highest levels of concentration and creativity— and scheduling them in the early hours when your energy is at its peak. For instance, if you have a project that demands deep focus, block out the first hour or two after your morning routine specifically for this task. Label this block as "Deep Work" or "Focus Time," and commit to avoiding distractions during this period.

Adjusting your time blocks is essential to making time-blocking work in real life. No day is identical, and unforeseen events or shifts in priorities can occur. Flexibility within your blocks allows you to adapt without feeling like your entire schedule is thrown off balance. For example, you might need to shorten or shift your original blocks if an urgent task arises. The key is to reassess your priorities and reallocate your remaining time effectively.

Throughout the morning, include short breaks between your blocks. These breaks are critical for maintaining focus and energy, as they prevent burnout and offer moments to recalibrate. For instance, after an hour of focused work, take a five to ten-minute break to step away from your workspace. Use this time to stretch, hydrate, or rest your mind before diving back into your next block.

Starting your day with time blocking through a well-structured morning routine involves setting a consistent wake-up time, aligning your blocks with your priorities, and maintaining the flexibility to adjust as needed. By thoughtfully planning your morning blocks, you create a productive rhythm that carries you through the rest of your day with clarity and purpose.

Managing Interruptions and Distractions:

Managing interruptions and distractions is one of the most challenging aspects of maintaining a successful time-blocking routine. Despite the best-laid plans, unexpected events can arise, potentially derailing your schedule and causing frustration. However, with the right strategies, you can mitigate these disruptions and keep your day on track.

First, it's important to recognize that interruptions and distractions are inevitable. Rather than aiming for a completely interruption-free day, focus on building resilience and adaptability into your schedule. One effective approach is to include buffer blocks in your daily plan. These are small chunks of time— perhaps 15 to 30 minutes— strategically placed between your primary time blocks. Buffer blocks act as a cushion, allowing you to handle unexpected tasks or minor delays without disrupting your entire schedule. For example, if an unplanned phone call or urgent request pops up, you can address it during a buffer block instead of sacrificing the time allocated for critical tasks.

Another key strategy is to set clear boundaries during your time blocks, especially during periods of deep focus. Communicate your availability to colleagues, friends, and family, letting them know when you will not be disturbed unless it's an emergency. Simple actions like setting your status to "Do Not Disturb" on communication apps, closing your office door, or using noise-canceling headphones can signal others that you're in a focused work mode. Additionally, turning off notifications on your devices during important blocks can significantly reduce the temptation to check emails, messages, or social media.

When interruptions occur, practice quick decision-making to determine whether they require immediate attention or can be deferred. Not every disruption needs to derail your current focus. For example, if a coworker approaches you with a non-urgent question, you might politely ask if you can address it later during a more suitable time block. This practice, often called "batching," helps you manage tasks more efficiently by grouping similar activities rather than scattering them throughout the day.

Consider your environment to further guard against distractions. Create a workspace that minimizes potential disruptions. This might involve organizing your desk to reduce clutter, positioning your workspace away from high-traffic areas, or using apps to block distracting websites during specific time blocks. A well-organized environment supports a focused mindset and helps maintain the integrity of your time blocks.

Lastly, practice mindfulness and self-awareness to recognize when you're being drawn into a distraction. Often, distractions are self-imposed, like the urge to check social media or respond to non-urgent emails. Developing the habit of pausing and asking yourself if the task at hand aligns with your current time block can help you stay on course. If you find your focus waning, it might indicate that you need a short break or that your current time block needs adjustment.

Managing interruptions and distractions in time blocking requires a proactive and flexible approach. By incorporating buffer blocks, setting boundaries, making quick decisions about disruptions, optimizing your environment, and practicing mindfulness, you can effectively navigate the unexpected while maintaining control over your time and productivity.

Adapting Time Blocks to Different Life Roles:

Adapting time blocks to different life roles is essential for creating a balanced and fulfilling daily routine. Each role you play— whether as a professional, a family member, a friend, or an individual focused on personal growth— demands time and attention. Customizing your time blocks to reflect these diverse roles ensures that none are neglected and your day aligns with your values and priorities.

Start by identifying your key life roles and the responsibilities associated with each. For most people, these roles can be broadly categorized into work, personal life, family time, and self-care. Each role has unique demands, so you can allocate your time more effectively by recognizing them. For instance, your work role might include meetings, project deadlines, and strategic planning, while your personal life might involve hobbies, social activities, or learning new skills.

Once you have identified your roles, consider the time and energy each one requires. Work-related time blocks might be concentrated during the traditional workday, where focus and productivity are paramount. These blocks can be tailored to your work tasks, ensuring you meet deadlines and achieve your professional goals. To maintain balance, it's crucial to set clear boundaries around these work blocks, ensuring they don't spill over into personal or family time.

Personal lifetime blocks are equally important and should be intentionally scheduled into your day. These blocks might include time for activities that bring you joy, relaxation, or personal development. Whether reading a book, engaging in a creative hobby, or catching up with friends, personal time blocks should be considered non-negotiable commitments to yourself. This ensures that you continue to nurture your passions and maintain a sense of individuality outside of work and family responsibilities.

Family time blocks are critical for nurturing relationships and creating meaningful connections with loved ones. These blocks should be designed around the needs and routines of your family members, whether it is having dinner together, helping with homework, or simply enjoying each other's company. Scheduling regular family time helps reinforce bonds and ensures that family relationships remain a priority, even amid a busy schedule.

Finally, self-care time blocks are essential for maintaining well-being. These blocks should be dedicated to activities that promote physical, mental, and emotional health, such as exercise, meditation, or simply unwinding. Self-care time is not just about relaxation; it is about recharging so you can show up fully in all your other roles. You build resilience and prevent burnout by prioritizing self-care in your time blocks.

As you customize your time blocks for each role, consider the natural rhythms of your day. Some roles require more attention in the morning, while others are better suited for the evening. For example, if you're most productive in the morning, you might schedule your most demanding work tasks and reserve the evening for personal activities or family time. Flexibility is key— your time blocks should evolve with your changing needs and priorities.

Adapting your time blocks to different life roles involves a thoughtful and intentional approach. By customizing your schedule to reflect the unique demands of work, personal life, family time, and self-care, you create a balanced routine that supports all aspects of your life. This holistic approach to time blocking ensures you fulfill your roles' responsibilities while making time for joy, connection, and personal well-being.

Chapter 6:
Overcoming Challenges with Time Blocking

Dealing with Procrastination:

Procrastination is a common challenge that can undermine even the most well-intentioned plans. However, time blocking can be a powerful tool in combating procrastination by providing structure, accountability, and motivation to stay on track.

One of the primary reasons people procrastinate is the overwhelming nature of certain tasks. When a project or task feels too large or daunting, it's easy to put it off in favor of more manageable activities. Time blocking addresses this by breaking down larger tasks into smaller, more manageable chunks. Instead of facing an entire project all at once, you can divide it into specific time blocks, each dedicated to a particular aspect of the task. This approach makes the task seem less intimidating and provides a clear path forward, reducing the urge to procrastinate.

Additionally, time blocking creates a sense of urgency and commitment. By assigning specific tasks to specific time slots, you make a mini-deadline for each task. Knowing that you've set aside a particular time to work on something encourages you to start, as delaying would mean disrupting your entire schedule. This sense of urgency can be particularly effective in countering procrastination, as it removes the open-ended nature of many tasks and replaces it with a concrete plan.

To further combat procrastination, it's helpful to start with a time block dedicated to the most challenging or least appealing task of the day—often referred to as "eating the frog." By tackling this task first, you get it out of the way early and build momentum for the rest of the day. Once you've completed the most difficult task, everything else feels more manageable, making it easier to stay on track.

Time blocking also helps you recognize and address the underlying reasons for procrastination. For instance, if you find yourself repeatedly avoiding a particular task, it might indicate that it is either too vague, too complex, or not aligned with your goals. By reflecting on your time blocks and identifying procrastination patterns, you can adjust— such as breaking the task down further, seeking additional resources, or reassessing its importance— to overcome these obstacles.

Another effective strategy is incorporating short, focused work sessions within your time blocks, such as using the Pomodoro Technique. This method involves working for a set amount of time (typically 25 minutes) followed by a short break. Knowing that you only need to focus for a limited period can reduce resistance and make starting easier. Over time, these small, consistent efforts can help you build the discipline to overcome procrastination.

Lastly, building rewards or positive reinforcement within your time blocks can enhance motivation. For example, after completing a particularly challenging task, you might reward yourself with a short break, a snack, or a quick walk. These small incentives can create a positive association with completing tasks, making it more likely that you'll start and finish what you've planned.

Time blocking is a valuable tool for combating procrastination. It breaks down tasks, creates urgency, addresses underlying issues, and builds discipline through structured work sessions. Using time blocking effectively, you can overcome procrastination and stay on track toward your goals.

Adjusting Blocks When Life Happens:

Life is unpredictable, and even the most meticulously planned time blocks can be disrupted by unexpected events. Whether it's a sudden meeting, an urgent personal matter, or just an off day, the key to maintaining productivity lies in adapting your time blocks while keeping your overall goals in sight.

The first step in being flexible with your time blocks is to accept that changes will happen. Embracing this reality allows you to approach your schedule with adaptability rather than rigidity. When an unexpected event occurs, recognize it as an opportunity to practice resilience and recalibrate your day instead of feeling frustrated or defeated.

One practical tip is to build flexibility into your schedule from the start. As mentioned in previous sections, including buffer blocks throughout your day can provide the necessary space to handle unforeseen events. These buffer blocks act as a safety net, allowing you to absorb delays or interruptions without significantly impacting your productivity. For instance, if a meeting runs over time, you can adjust your subsequent tasks without causing a domino effect of missed deadlines.

When life throws a curve ball, it's essential to prioritize. Evaluate the remaining tasks in your schedule and determine which ones are most critical to accomplish that day. If you need to, adjust your time blocks to focus on these high-priority tasks while deferring less urgent ones to another day. This prioritization ensures you continue progressing on your most important goals, even if your day doesn't go as planned.

Another tip for adjusting time blocks is to practice task batching. If your schedule is unexpectedly shortened, look for opportunities to combine similar tasks into a single block. For example, if you had separate time blocks for responding to emails and making phone calls, you could merge them into one communication block. This allows you to maintain productivity by tackling multiple related tasks within a condensed time frame.

Having a backup plan for your most critical time blocks is also helpful. Identify alternative times or days when you could complete these tasks if your original plan is disrupted. A backup plan provides peace of mind and a clear path forward, even when things are unexpected.

In some cases, it may be necessary to let go of less important tasks to maintain focus on what truly matters. Consider what can be postponed, delegated, or eliminated from your schedule if your day is derailed. By being strategic about what you can let go of, you free up time and mental energy to concentrate on the tasks that align most closely with your goals.

Finally, practice self-compassion and flexibility with yourself. Not every day will go perfectly, and that's okay. The ability to adjust your time blocks with grace is a sign of a well-rounded, adaptable approach to productivity. Rather than seeing adjustments as failures, consider them a testament to your ability to stay productive in life's unpredictability.

Adjusting your time blocks when life happens involves embracing flexibility, prioritizing tasks, using buffer blocks, batching tasks, having backup plans, and practicing self-compassion. You can maintain productivity even when your day does not go as planned, ensuring you stay on track toward your larger goals.

Maintaining Consistency and Motivation:

Maintaining consistency and motivation with time blocking over the long term can be challenging, especially as the initial excitement wears off or as your routine becomes more familiar. However, with the right techniques, you can keep time blocking fresh and effective.

One of the most effective ways to maintain consistency is to establish a routine that you can easily integrate into your daily life. Start by setting up a regular time to review and plan your time blocks, whether at the end of each day, at the beginning of the week, or during a quiet moment on the weekend. This habit of regular planning helps reinforce the importance of time blocking and ensures that it becomes a natural part of your workflow rather than an additional task.

To keep motivation high, it is crucial to celebrate your successes and recognize the progress you've made. After completing a series of time blocks or achieving a significant milestone, take a moment to reflect on what you've accomplished. This could be as simple as acknowledging how much you've gotten done or treating yourself to something you enjoy. Celebrating your wins reinforces positive behavior and makes you more likely to continue with the practice.

Another technique to sustain motivation is periodically refreshing your approach to time blocking. Over time, your needs and priorities may change, and so should your time blocks. Regularly assess what is working and what is not, and be open to experimenting with new methods or tools. For example, suppose your current system is becoming stale. In that case, introduce a new digital tool, redesign your time block categories, or adjust the duration of your blocks to suit your energy levels better.

Incorporating variety into your time blocks can also help keep things fresh. For instance, if you've been using the same structure for a while, consider mixing up your routine by varying the order of tasks, introducing new projects, or scheduling creative or leisure activities as part of your day. This variety prevents monotony and can rekindle your interest in the time-blocking process.

Accountability can play a significant role in maintaining consistency. Share your time-blocking goals with a colleague, friend, or mentor who can check in periodically. This external accountability adds a layer of motivation, as you will be more likely to stick with your time blocks, knowing that someone else is aware of your goals.

It is also essential to remain flexible and compassionate with yourself. There will be days when sticking to your time blocks feels more difficult, and that's perfectly normal. Instead of viewing these moments as failures, treat them as opportunities to learn and adjust. Allow yourself the grace to adapt your time blocks when necessary, understanding that consistency doesn't mean perfection— it means showing up regularly and doing your best.

Lastly, reconnect with your "why." Remind yourself of the reasons you started time-blocking in the first place. Whether to achieve better work-life balance, increase productivity, or reduce stress, keeping your core motivations in mind can help you stay committed to the practice over the long term. When you're clear on the benefits and purpose behind time blocking, it becomes easier to maintain the discipline needed to continue.

Maintaining consistency and motivation with time blocking involves establishing a regular planning routine, celebrating successes, refreshing your approach, incorporating variety, seeking accountability, practicing flexibility, and reconnecting with your underlying motivations. These techniques ensure that time blocking remains a valuable and dynamic tool in your productivity arsenal, helping you stay on track and engaged over the long term.

Chapter 7:
Advanced Time Blocking Strategies

Time Blocking for Deep Work:

Time blocking for deep work is one of the most powerful strategies to tackle complex, high-impact tasks that demand deep concentration and creativity. As defined by productivity expert Cal Newport, deep work refers to activities performed in a focused, distraction-free concentration that pushes your cognitive abilities to their limit. These tasks significantly move the needle in your personal and professional life, and time blocking can help you carve out the space needed to accomplish them.

The first step in using time blocking for deep work is identifying the tasks that qualify as deep work. These tasks, such as writing, strategic planning, coding, or problem-solving, require your full attention and are often intellectually demanding. Once you've identified these tasks, prioritize them within your schedule, ideally when you're most alert and capable of sustained focus. This is in the morning for many people, but it can vary depending on your natural energy rhythms.

When blocking out time for deep work, allocating uninterrupted blocks of at least 90 minutes to two hours is essential. Shorter time blocks often aren't sufficient for achieving the concentration required for deep work, as it takes time to immerse yourself fully in complex tasks. During these blocks, eliminate all distractions by turning off notifications, closing unnecessary tabs on your computer, and setting your phone to "Do Not Disturb." Let others know you're unavailable during this time to avoid interruptions.

Creating a ritual around deep work time blocks can also enhance focus and productivity. This could involve starting your deep work session with a specific routine, such as clearing your workspace, making a cup of tea, or spending a few minutes reviewing your goals for the session.

These rituals signal to your brain that it's time to transition into deep work mode, helping you settle into a state of focus more quickly.

Managing your energy levels to sustain your concentration during these deep work blocks is important. This might involve taking a short break after a particularly intense period of work, practicing mindfulness or breathing exercises to reset your focus, or even stepping outside for a few minutes to clear your mind. Regularly scheduled breaks can help prevent mental fatigue, allowing you to maintain high productivity levels throughout your deep work sessions.

Another advanced strategy is combining time blocking with batching similar deep work tasks. By grouping related functions into a single time block, you minimize the cognitive load required to switch between different types of thinking. For example, if you're working on multiple sections of a report, dedicate a deep work block to focus exclusively on writing, then another block later for revising or editing. This approach helps maintain momentum and keeps you deeply engaged with the task.

Finally, review and refine your deep work blocks regularly. After each session, take a few moments to reflect on what worked well and what could be improved. Did you manage to stay focused the entire time? Were there any interruptions or distractions that could be better mitigated? Use these insights to optimize future deep work sessions, continually honing your ability to enter and sustain deep focus.

Time blocking for deep work involves prioritizing high-impact tasks, dedicating long, uninterrupted blocks of time to them, eliminating distractions, creating rituals, managing energy levels, batching similar tasks, and regularly reviewing your approach. By mastering these strategies, you can leverage the full power of deep work to achieve your most significant goals.

Batching Similar Tasks:

Batching similar tasks is an advanced time-blocking strategy that can significantly boost your efficiency by minimizing the cognitive load associated with task-switching. When you group functions of a similar nature into the same time block, you streamline your workflow, reduce the time spent transitioning between different types of activities, and maintain a focused state of mind.

The concept behind batching is simple: tasks that require similar thought processes or tools are grouped and completed in a single, dedicated time block. This approach contrasts with a more fragmented schedule where unrelated tasks are scattered throughout the day, leading to frequent shifts in focus and productivity losses. For example, instead of checking emails, making phone calls, and drafting a report all in separate, scattered time slots, you could batch all your communication tasks (emails and calls) into one block and reserve another for focused writing.

The benefits of batching similar tasks are twofold. First, it minimizes the cognitive cost of context switching. Each time you switch from one type of task to another— from creative writing to data analysis— your brain needs time to adjust to the new kind of thinking required. Though often subtle, this adjustment period can add up over the day, reducing productivity and increasing mental fatigue. Focusing on one task at a time eliminates the need for constant mental reorientation.

Second, batching allows you to take advantage of momentum. Once you get into the groove of a particular task, it becomes easier to maintain that momentum and complete similar tasks more quickly and efficiently. For instance, if you're responding to emails, you might find that after the first few, you develop a rhythm that makes the rest easier to tackle. This momentum can be lost if you interrupt the flow to switch to a completely different task, only to return to emails later.

To implement batching effectively, start by identifying the types of tasks you regularly perform that can be grouped. Common examples include administrative tasks (like responding to emails, scheduling meetings, and filing documents), creative tasks (such as writing, designing, or brainstorming), and analytical tasks (like reviewing data, conducting research, or financial planning). Once you've identified these groups, allocate specific time blocks dedicated solely to each category.

Setting up your environment to support your batched tasks is also helpful. For example, during a block for creative work, you might close all unnecessary tabs on your computer, put your phone on silent, and have any materials you need at hand. This ensures you can dive straight into the task once you start your time block without additional preparation.

While batching is highly effective, it is important to remain flexible. Some tasks might not fit neatly into a batch, or unexpected events may require you to adjust your plan. In these cases, try to maintain the integrity of your batches as much as possible, but be willing to adapt when necessary.

Batching similar tasks into dedicated time blocks maximizes efficiency by reducing cognitive load, minimizing context switching, and allowing you to build and maintain momentum. By grouping tasks that require similar skills or tools, you streamline your workflow, making it easier to focus and complete your work effectively.

Time Blocking for Teams:

Time blocking presents a unique opportunity for teams to enhance collaboration and individual productivity within a group setting. When implemented effectively, time blocking can help teams align their efforts, reduce unnecessary interruptions, and create a structured environment where group work and individual tasks can thrive.

The first step in implementing time blocking for teams is establishing a shared understanding of its purpose and benefits. Team members need to recognize how time blocking can help them manage their workloads more efficiently while still allowing for necessary collaboration. This can be achieved through a group discussion or a workshop where the principles of time blocking are introduced and tailored to the team's specific needs.

Once the team is on board, it is important to identify and agree upon core collaboration times. These are blocks of time where team members can work together on shared tasks, attend meetings, or engage in brainstorming sessions. By designating specific periods for collaboration, teams can minimize interruptions during other blocks of time, allowing individuals to focus on their tasks without the constant expectation of being immediately available.

For example, a team might agree that mornings are dedicated to individual deep work, where each member focuses on their high-priority tasks without interruption. Afternoons could then be reserved for meetings, collaborative projects, and communication. This structure ensures that everyone can engage in focused work and teamwork without impeding the other.

To further support individual productivity within a team setting, it is essential to encourage team members to create time blocks for personal tasks. These blocks should align with the team schedule and allow flexibility based on individual work styles and responsibilities. For instance, while the team might collectively decide on afternoon collaboration, individual members could still time block their specific tasks during these periods, ensuring they remain productive while being available for teamwork.

Another key aspect of implementing time blocking for teams is clear communication. Regular check-ins, either daily or weekly, can help the team stay aligned and adjust time blocks as needed. During these check-ins, team members can discuss progress, challenges, and whether the current time-blocking structure works effectively. This ongoing communication ensures that the time-blocking strategy remains dynamic and responsive to the team's evolving needs.

It is also important to consider using shared tools and platforms that facilitate time blocking in a team environment. Tools like shared calendars, project management software, or time-blocking apps can help synchronize schedules, making it easier for everyone to see when colleagues are available for collaboration or deep work. This transparency fosters a sense of accountability and helps avoid scheduling conflicts that could disrupt productivity.

Finally, flexibility should be built into the team's time-blocking approach. While structure is crucial, there will inevitably be times when the team needs to adapt to changing priorities or unforeseen circumstances. Encouraging a culture where time blocks can be adjusted when necessary without sacrificing overall productivity ensures that the team can remain agile and responsive.

Time blocking for teams involves establishing core collaboration times, encouraging individual time blocks, maintaining clear communication, using shared tools for synchronization, and remaining flexible. By implementing these strategies, teams can create a balanced environment supporting collaboration and individual productivity, leading to more efficient and effective outcomes.

Chapter 8:
Case Studies and Success Stories

Real-Life Examples of Time-Blocking Success:

Case Studies and Success Stories will explore real-life examples of how individuals and organizations have successfully implemented time blocking to achieve significant goals. These profiles provide tangible evidence of the effectiveness of time-stopping, offering inspiration and practical insights for readers looking to apply these strategies in their lives.

One compelling example comes from the world of tech startups, where time blocking has become a crucial tool for managing rapid growth and complex projects. A case in point is a mid-sized software company struggling to balance product development, client relations, and internal operations. By introducing time blocking across the organization, they could allocate specific blocks of time for different functions— such as morning blocks for coding and product development, followed by afternoon blocks for meetings and client interactions. This structured approach improved productivity and reduced employee burnout, as team members could focus on one task at a time without constant interruptions.

On an individual level, consider the story of a freelance graphic designer who used time blocking to juggle multiple client projects while maintaining a healthy work-life balance. Initially, the designer found it difficult to switch between creative tasks for different clients and often felt overwhelmed by the demands of managing a freelance business. By adopting time blocking, the designer created dedicated time slots for each client, ensuring focused attention on each project without the stress of multitasking. Additionally, the designer reserved time blocks for business development, marketing, and personal activities, which helped sustain both professional growth and individual well-being.

Another inspiring example comes from a university professor who used time blocking to enhance productivity in both teaching and research. Faced with balancing lecture preparation, student consultations, and academic writing, the professor implemented time blocking to create distinct periods for each responsibility. Morning blocks were dedicated to research and writing, ensuring that deep work could be accomplished without interruption. Teaching preparation and student meetings were scheduled in the afternoons, allowing the professors to be fully present for their students. This approach improved the quality of the professor's work and led to more publications and better student engagement.

In the corporate world, a large multinational company successfully implemented time blocking to streamline its project management processes. With teams across different time zones, the company faced challenges coordinating efforts and ensuring consistent progress. By standardizing time blocking across all teams, they created synchronized work schedules that facilitated collaboration while respecting individual team members' focus time. For instance, the first two hours of each day were set aside for deep work, followed by a block for team meetings and cross-departmental updates. This approach led to faster project completion times and improved communication, as everyone knew when to expect conferences and focus on their tasks.

These case studies highlight the versatility and effectiveness of time blocking across different contexts. Whether it is a tech startup, a freelancer, an academic professional, or a large corporation, time blocking has proven to be a powerful tool for managing time, reducing stress, and achieving individual and organizational goals. From these real-life examples, readers can learn how they might adapt time blocking to fit their unique circumstances, leading to greater productivity and success.

Lessons Learned from the Pros:

When mastering time blocking, productivity experts offer wisdom from years of experience and research. Their insights provide valuable lessons to help anyone refine their time-blocking practices to achieve greater efficiency, focus, and balance. Here are some key takeaways and advice from the pros:

1. Start Small and Be Consistent
One of the most common advice from productivity experts is to start small. Instead of overhauling your entire schedule with time blocks, begin by time-blocking just one or two critical tasks each day. This approach helps you gradually adapt to the new system without feeling overwhelmed. As you become more comfortable with time blocking, you can expand its use to cover more aspects of your day. Consistency is crucial— by regularly using time blocks, you'll see the cumulative benefits in your productivity and stress levels.

2. Protect Your Deep Work Time
Cal Newport, the author of "Deep Work," emphasizes the importance of protecting time blocks dedicated to deep work. You achieve your most significant accomplishments during focused, uninterrupted work. Newport advises setting aside specific times each day for deep work and guarding these blocks from interruptions and distractions. This might involve turning off notifications, setting boundaries with colleagues, or finding a quiet workplace space. Treating your deep work blocks as sacred, non-negotiable appointments with yourself is the key.

3. Flexibility is Key
Laura Vanderkam, a time management expert and author of "168 Hours," advocates for flexibility within your time-blocking system. While structure is essential, it's equally important to recognize that life is unpredictable. Vanderkam suggests building flexibility into your schedule by including buffer blocks and being willing to adjust your time blocks as needed. This approach prevents you from feeling trapped by your schedule and allows you to adapt to changing circumstances without losing momentum.

4. Prioritize High-Value Tasks
Stephen Covey, author of "The 7 Habits of Highly Effective People," stresses the importance of prioritizing tasks that align with your long-term goals. In the context of time blocking, this means identifying your most important tasks (MITs) and ensuring they receive prime time

blocks in your schedule. Covey's advice to "put first things first" encourages you to focus on tasks with the most significant impact rather than getting bogged down by less critical activities.

5. Reflect and Adjust Regularly
Productivity experts often recommend regular reflection as part of the time-blocking process. David Allen, the creator of the "Getting Things Done" (GTD) methodology, advises a weekly review where you assess your past week's time blocks, celebrate successes, and identify areas for improvement. This practice allows you to refine your approach, ensuring that your time-blocking strategy remains aligned with your goals and current priorities.

6. Embrace Technology Wisely
Many experts, including Tim Ferriss, author of "The 4-Hour Workweek," highlight the importance of using technology to enhance time blocking but caution against becoming overly reliant on it. Ferriss suggests using digital tools to automate and streamline your time-blocking process— such as calendar apps or project management software — but warns against the potential distraction of constant connectivity. The advice here is to choose tools that support your time blocking without adding unnecessary complexity or distractions.

7. Balance Work with Rest
Productivity experts like Tony Schwartz, co-author of "The Power of Full Engagement," emphasize the importance of balancing work with rest. Schwartz advocates for a rhythm of intense focus followed by rest, which can be effectively implemented through time blocking. You maintain your energy and prevent burnout by scheduling regular breaks and ensuring your time blocks include downtime. This balance is essential for sustaining productivity over the long term.

The key lessons from productivity experts about time blocking include starting small, protecting deep work time, maintaining flexibility, prioritizing high-value tasks, reflecting regularly, embracing technology wisely, and balancing work with rest. These insights provide a strong foundation for optimizing their time-blocking strategy and achieving lasting success.

Chapter 9:
Adapting Time Blocking Over Time

Evolving Your Time Blocks:

As your life and work evolve, so too should your time-blocking system. What works today might not be as effective in a few months or years, so it is crucial to regularly revisit and refine your time blocks to ensure they continue to meet your needs and help you achieve your goals.

The first step in evolving your time blocks is to schedule regular reviews of your system. This could be monthly, quarterly, or even annual, depending on the pace of change in your life and work. During these reviews, assess how well your current time blocks are working. Are they helping you stay productive and focused? Are you consistently able to complete your most important tasks? If not, it may be time to make adjustments.

One of the key indicators that your time blocks need refining is a shift in your priorities. As your personal and professional goals evolve, the tasks that require your attention will likely change. For example, if you've recently taken on a new role at work, you may need to allocate more time to learning new skills or managing a team. Similarly, changes in your personal life— such as starting a new hobby, managing a family, or pursuing further education— may require you to adjust your time blocks to accommodate these new commitments.

Another factor to consider is your energy levels throughout the day. Over time, you might notice that your peak productivity periods have shifted or that certain tasks require more or less time than before. Pay attention to these changes and adjust your time blocks accordingly. For instance, if your most creative work now happens in the late afternoon instead of the morning, shift your deep work blocks to align with this new pattern.

Flexibility is also essential as you refine your time-blocking system. While the structure provided by time blocking is valuable, it is important to remain open to experimentation. If you are not achieving the desired results, try varying the length of your time blocks, experimenting with different types of tasks within the same block, or even trying new tools and techniques to support your time management. This iterative approach ensures that your time-blocking system continues to evolve in response to your changing needs.

Incorporating feedback from others can also be valuable in evolving your time blocks. If you work in a team or regularly interact with colleagues, clients, or family members, consider their perspectives on how your time management affects them. Adjusted time blocks could handle certain collaborative tasks more efficiently, or there are opportunities to streamline communication and reduce unnecessary meetings.

It is also important to recognize when a complete overhaul of your time-blocking system is necessary. Life events such as moving to a new city, starting a new job, or undergoing major life changes like having a child or returning to school might require you to rethink your approach. In these cases, start from the ground up, re-evaluating your goals, priorities, and available time before rebuilding your time blocks to suit your new circumstances.

Lastly, remember that evolving your time blocks is an ongoing process. Your time-blocking system should grow and change with you as you continue to grow and change. Keep the lines of communication open between yourself and your schedule— regularly asking what's working, what's not, and what could be improved— so that your time blocks remain a dynamic tool for achieving your goals.

Evolving your time blocks involves regular reviews, adjusting to shifting priorities and energy levels, maintaining flexibility, incorporating feedback, and being willing to overhaul your system completely when necessary. Continuously refining your time-blocking system ensures it remains effective and aligned with your evolving life and work.

Time Blocking for Different Seasons of Life:

Time blocking is not a one-size-fits-all approach; it must be adapted to suit the different seasons of life you may go through, whether you're a student, professional, parent, or retiree. Each phase comes with its unique demands, and your time-blocking strategy should evolve to meet these changing needs, ensuring that you continue to use your time effectively while balancing your various responsibilities and aspirations.

For students, time blocking is particularly valuable for managing the demands of coursework, extracurricular activities, and social life. In this phase, the key challenge is often balancing academic responsibilities with personal interests and rest. A student's time-blocking schedule might include dedicated blocks for attending classes, studying, and completing assignments, with additional time for hobbies, part-time work, and socializing. Flexibility is crucial, as students often face fluctuating workloads and deadlines. Time blocks should be adjusted regularly to accommodate exam periods, project deadlines, and other academic priorities while still allowing time for relaxation and self-care.

As a professional, time blocking becomes essential for managing career-related tasks, personal development, and work-life balance. In this phase, it's important to prioritize time blocks for deep work, meetings, and professional growth while also allocating time for personal life, including health, relationships, and leisure. Professionals often face the challenge of juggling multiple projects and responsibilities, making it crucial to distinguish between high-priority tasks and less urgent ones. Time blocks should be structured to ensure critical work is completed during peak productivity hours, with flexibility to handle unexpected tasks or priority changes.

Time blocking can be a lifesaver for parents in managing the competing demands of work, family, and personal time. Parenting often requires a high degree of flexibility, as unexpected events and changes in routine are common. Parents might use time blocks to schedule work tasks around school drop-offs, pick-ups, and other family responsibilities. It's also important to block out time for family activities, such as meals, playtime, and outings, while ensuring that personal time for rest, exercise, and hobbies is not neglected. Time blocking can help parents maintain balance and control, even amid a busy and unpredictable schedule.

For retirees, time blocking takes a different focus, shifting from career and family obligations to personal fulfillment and leisure. In this phase of life, the challenge is often finding meaningful ways to fill time while maintaining a sense of purpose and engagement. Retirees might use time blocking to structure their days around hobbies, volunteer work, social activities, and physical exercise. Time blocks can also be used to explore new interests, travel, or pursue lifelong learning opportunities. The emphasis is on creating a balanced schedule that promotes well-being and enjoyment while allowing for the flexibility that retirement affords.

In each phase, the common thread is the need to adapt your time-blocking strategy to fit the specific demands and priorities of your current season of life. What works well during one phase may need to be completely rethought as you transition into another. Regularly reassessing your goals, responsibilities, and available time ensures that your time-blocking system continues to serve you effectively, no matter where you are.

Time blocking should be tailored to the different seasons of life, whether you are a student balancing academic and personal demands, a professional managing career and personal growth, a parent juggling work and family responsibilities, or a retiree seeking fulfillment and engagement. By adapting your time-blocking approach to suit your current phase, you can maintain productivity, balance, and satisfaction throughout your life.

Preparing for the Future:

As we look to the future, technological advancements and societal changes will continue to reshape how we live and work. To ensure that your time-blocking system remains relevant and effective in the face of these changes, it is important to adopt a forward-thinking approach that anticipates and adapts to new developments.

One of the most significant influences on time management in the future is the continued integration of technology into our daily lives. From AI-powered productivity tools to the increasing prevalence of remote work, these changes will require a time-blocking system that is both flexible and tech-savvy. To prepare for this, consider embracing digital tools that can enhance time blocking, such as apps that sync across devices, offer AI-driven scheduling suggestions, or automate routine tasks. Staying up-to-date with the latest tools and platforms can help you maintain a streamlined and efficient approach to managing your time.

However, balancing leveraging technology and avoiding overreliance on it is also important. As technology evolves, so too can the risks of distraction and burnout, particularly if we become too dependent on digital tools that demand constant attention. To counter this, consider incorporating regular digital detoxes into your time-blocking routine, where you set aside time blocks specifically for offline activities. This helps maintain focus and ensures that your time-blocking system remains grounded in real-world priorities rather than entirely dictated by digital inputs.

Societal changes, such as shifts in work culture, the rise of gig and freelance economies, and changing family dynamics, will also impact how we approach time management. For instance, as more people adopt flexible work arrangements, the traditional 9-to-5 time blocks may become less relevant. To stay ahead of these trends, it is important to cultivate a flexible mindset that allows you to adjust your time-blocking system to fit new work patterns. This might involve creating time blocks accommodating unconventional work hours or balancing multiple income streams with personal and family life.

In addition to these external changes, it is important to consider the long-term sustainability of your time-blocking system. Your time blocks should evolve as your responsibilities, goals, and interests evolve. Regularly revisiting and refining your time-blocking strategy ensures that it aligns with your current and future needs. This might mean reevaluating your time blocks annually or whenever you experience significant life changes, such as a career shift, relocation, or major personal milestones.

Building resilience into your time-blocking system by preparing for potential disruptions is also beneficial. This could involve developing contingency plans for unexpected events like health issues, economic downturns, or technological failures. By anticipating these possibilities and creating flexible time blocks that allow quick adjustments, you can maintain productivity even in uncertainty.

Finally, staying informed about emerging trends in time management and productivity can help you keep your time-blocking system relevant. This might involve following thought leaders in the field, attending workshops, or engaging with communities that share innovative time management strategies. By continuously learning and adapting, you can ensure that your time-blocking system remains effective in navigating the challenges and opportunities of the future.

Preparing for the future involves embracing technology while maintaining balance, staying flexible in response to societal changes, regularly refining your time blocks, building resilience for potential disruptions, and staying informed about emerging trends. By taking these proactive steps, you can ensure that your time-blocking system remains a powerful tool for managing your time effectively, no matter what the future holds.

Conclusion

The Long-Term Benefits of Time Blocking:

As we conclude our exploration of time blocking, it is essential to reflect on the long-term benefits that this powerful practice can bring into your life. Time blocking is more than just a method for organizing your day; it is a comprehensive strategy that, when implemented consistently, can lead to sustained productivity, a better work-life balance, and a deeper sense of personal fulfillment.

One of the most significant long-term benefits of time blocking is its ability to foster sustained productivity. You create a structured environment where focus and efficiency naturally thrive by dedicating specific time blocks to your most important tasks. Over time, this consistent application of focused effort allows you to accomplish more in less time, reducing the mental fatigue that often accompanies a chaotic or unstructured schedule. As your productivity increases, so does your capacity to take on new challenges and opportunities, propelling you toward long-term goals with greater momentum.

In addition to boosting productivity, time blocking plays a crucial role in achieving a better work-life balance. In today's fast-paced world, it's too easy to let work spill over into personal time, leading to burnout and strained relationships. Time blocking offers a solution by clearly delineating time for work, family, individual pursuits, and rest. Honoring these boundaries ensures that each aspect of your life receives the attention it deserves, allowing you to be fully present in whatever you do. This balance enhances your overall well-being and improves the quality of your work and personal life as you approach each area with renewed energy and focus.

Perhaps most importantly, time blocking contributes to deeper personal fulfillment. Controlling your time can align your daily actions with your core values and long-term aspirations. Whether making progress on a passion project, spending quality time with loved ones, or investing in your personal growth, time blocking ensures that your days reflect what truly matters to you. This alignment between your actions and values creates a sense of purpose and satisfaction that transcends the daily hustle, leading to a more fulfilling and meaningful life.

Furthermore, the discipline and intentionality fostered by time blocking can have ripple effects on other areas of your life. As you become more adept at managing your time, you may be better equipped to handle stress, make decisions, and pursue your goals with clarity and confidence. This holistic improvement in your life enhances personal and professional success and improves inner peace and contentment.

The long-term benefits of time blocking are profound and far-reaching. By cultivating sustained productivity, achieving a better work-life balance, and aligning your daily actions with your deeper values, time blocking empowers you to lead a life that is not only more organized and efficient but also more fulfilling and meaningful. As you refine and adapt your time-blocking system, you'll discover that investing time and effort in this practice pays dividends in every aspect of your life, helping you truly live your life on your terms.

Encouragement to Start Your Time-Blocking Journey:

As we wrap up this journey through the art and science of time blocking, I want to leave you with a final word of encouragement: the time to start is now. Time blocking can be the key to unlocking your full potential, no matter where you are in life— whether you are a student, a professional, a parent, or someone navigating life transitions.

It is natural to feel daunted by the prospect of reorganizing your life around time blocks, especially if you've never tried a structured time management system. But remember, time blocking is not about perfection but progress. The beauty of time blocking lies in its flexibility and adaptability. You do not have to get it right on the first try, and there is no one-size-fits-all approach. The most important step is to begin.

Start small, with just a few time blocks each day, focusing on your most important tasks. As you experience the clarity and focus from dedicated time blocks, you will find it easier to expand the practice into other areas of your life. Each day is an opportunity to refine your approach, experiment with what works best for you, and see real progress in managing your time.

The rewards of time blocking are well worth the effort. As your productivity increases, your stress decreases, and your life becomes more balanced, you will realize that time blocking isn't just a time management tool but a pathway to a more intentional, fulfilling life. It's a way to take control of your most valuable resource— your time— and use it to build the life you truly want.

So take that first step. Create your first-time block today, even if it is just for 30 minutes. Use it to focus on something important that moves you closer to your goals. And then, keep going. Each block of time you set aside is an investment in your future, your dreams, and the person you want to become.

The journey of a thousand miles begins with a single step. Let today be that step for you. Start your time-blocking journey now, and watch as it transforms your days and life. You have the power to shape your time and, in doing so, to shape your destiny. The possibilities are endless, and it all begins with a single, intentional block of time.

Appendices

Glossary of Terms

Buffer Block: A specific time block to handle unexpected tasks, delays, or interruptions. It acts as a cushion in your schedule, providing flexibility without disrupting your overall plan.

Context Switching: The mental process of shifting attention from one task to another. Frequent context switching can lead to reduced productivity and increased cognitive load, making time blocking an effective strategy to minimize it.

Deep Work: A concept popularized by Cal Newport, referring to periods of focused, uninterrupted work on tasks that require significant cognitive effort. Deep work blocks are critical for accomplishing high-impact tasks.

Digital Detox: A period during which you intentionally disconnect from digital devices and online platforms. Digital detoxes can be scheduled as time blocks to reduce stress and improve focus.

Eisenhower Matrix: A time management tool that helps prioritize tasks based on urgency and importance. It is often used with time blocking to determine which tasks should be scheduled into your time blocks.

Flex Time Blocks: Time blocks intentionally left open or loosely defined to accommodate changes in your schedule or allow for spontaneous activities.

High-Priority Tasks (MITs): These are critical to achieving your goals and should be prioritized in your time-blocking schedule. MIT stands for Most Important Tasks.

Pomodoro Technique: A time management method that involves working for a set period (usually 25 minutes) followed by a short break. This technique can be incorporated into time blocking to maintain focus and productivity.

Time Blocking: A time management strategy that involves dividing your day into blocks of time, each dedicated to specific tasks or activities. Time blocking helps create structure, reduce distractions, and improve focus.

Time Batching: Grouping similar tasks into a single time block to maximize efficiency and minimize the cognitive load of switching between different types of activities.

Unstructured Time: Intentionally left open periods that were not planned or scheduled. Unstructured time allows for flexibility, creativity, and spontaneous activities.

Work-life balance is the equilibrium between work responsibilities and personal life, ensuring that neither dominates the other. Time blocking can help improve work-life balance by clearly defining when work ends and personal time begins.

WIP Limits (Work in Progress Limits): A concept often used in Kanban and Agile methodologies to limit the number of tasks in progress at any given time. WIP limits can be applied to time blocking to ensure your focus is not too thin across multiple tasks.

These terms and concepts form the foundation of the time-blocking strategy discussed in this book. Understanding and applying them will help you make the most of your time and lead a more organized, productive, and fulfilling life.

Recommended Resources

To further deepen your understanding of time management and productivity, here's a list of recommended books, podcasts, and online courses that offer valuable insights and practical advice.

Books
1. **"Deep Work" by Cal Newport**
   This book explores deep work— focused, uninterrupted periods of productivity— and provides strategies for cultivating this practice in daily life.

2. **"The 7 Habits of Highly Effective People" by Stephen Covey**
   A classic in personal development, this book introduces key principles for achieving personal and professional effectiveness, including time management strategies.

3. **"Atomic Habits" by James Clear**
   Clear's book offers a detailed look at how small habits can significantly change your life. It's particularly useful for understanding how to build and maintain productive routines.

4. **"Getting Things Done: The Art of Stress-Free Productivity" by David Allen**
   David Allen's GTD methodology is a comprehensive system for managing tasks and projects, making it an excellent companion to time blocking.

5. **"Make Time: How to Focus on What Matters Every Day" by Jake Knapp and John Zeratsky**
   This book provides practical techniques for creating time in your day for the things that matter most, complementing the time-blocking approach.

6. **"Essentialism: The Disciplined Pursuit of Less" by Greg McKeown**
   McKeown's book focuses on the importance of doing less but better, offering insights on prioritizing and eliminating non-essential tasks from your schedule.

Podcasts

1. **"The Productivity Show" by Asian Efficiency**
   This podcast covers productivity topics, including time blocking, goal setting, and habit formation, with actionable tips and expert interviews.

2. **"The Tim Ferriss Show" by Tim Ferriss**
   Tim Ferriss interviews top performers from various fields, exploring their routines, tools, and strategies for productivity, including time management techniques.

3. **"Deep Questions" by Cal Newport**
   In this podcast, Cal Newport explores questions about work, technology, and productivity, offering insights that align closely with the principles of time blocking.

4. **"Beyond the To-Do List" by Erik Fisher**
   This podcast features conversations with productivity experts and thought leaders, providing practical advice on managing tasks and improving efficiency.

5. **"The Focused Podcast" by David Sparks and Mike Schmitz**
   This podcast discusses strategies for maintaining focus and productivity in a world of distractions, including time blocking and other methods.

Online Courses

1. **"Getting Things Done" by David Allen on LinkedIn Learning**
   This course provides a comprehensive overview of the GTD methodology and offers practical implementation tips.

2. **"Productivity Masterclass: Create a Custom System that Works" by Thomas Frank on Skillshare**
   Thomas Frank's course guides you through building a personalized productivity system, incorporating time management techniques like time blocking.

3. **"Time Management Fundamentals" by Dave Crenshaw on LinkedIn Learning**
   This course covers the essentials of time management, including prioritizing tasks, managing your schedule, and avoiding common time-wasters.

4. **"Deep Work: Rules for Focused Success in a Distracted World" by Cal Newport on Udemy**
   Based on his book, this course teaches you how to cultivate deep work habits and apply them to achieve greater productivity and success.

5. **"The Science of Well-Being" by Yale University on Coursera**
   While not exclusively about time management, this course explores the science of happiness and productivity, providing insights that can enhance your time-blocking practice.

These resources offer knowledge and practical advice to help you improve your time management skills and overall productivity. By exploring these books, podcasts, and courses, you can deepen your understanding of the principles discussed in this book and further refine your approach to time blocking.

Examples

To help you start with time blocking, here are sample time block schedules for different days, including a typical workday, a weekend day, and a day with a mix of work and personal commitments. These templates are designed to be flexible, allowing you to adjust them according to your specific needs and priorities.

Sample Workday Schedule

6:00 AM – 7:00 AM: Morning Routine

- Activities: Wake up, exercise, shower, breakfast, and plan the day.
- Purpose: Set a positive tone for the day and prepare mentally and physically for the tasks ahead.

7:00 AM – 9:00 AM: Deep Work

- Activities: Focus on the most important task of the day (e.g., writing, coding, strategic planning).
- Purpose: Utilize peak energy levels for high-impact, cognitively demanding work.

9:00 AM – 10:00 AM: Email and Communication

- Activities: Check and respond to emails, messages, and voicemails.
- Purpose: Handle communication tasks efficiently without allowing them to interrupt deep work.

10:00 AM – 12:00 PM: Project Work

- Activities: Continue working on key projects or tasks that require focused attention.
- Purpose: Make significant progress on important projects.

12:00 PM – 1:00 PM: Lunch and Break

- Activities: Take a lunch break, walk, or engage in a relaxing activity.
- Purpose: Recharge and refresh for the second half of the day.

1:00 PM – 3:00 PM: Meetings/Collaborative Work

- Activities: Attend scheduled meetings, brainstorming sessions, or collaborative projects.
- Purpose: Engage in team activities and decision-making processes.

3:00 PM – 4:00 PM: Administrative Tasks

- Activities: Handle routine tasks such as filing, organizing, or updating reports.
- Purpose: Take care of essential but less demanding tasks.

4:00 PM – 5:00 PM: Buffer Block/Wrap-Up

- Activities: Address any overflow from earlier tasks, review the day's progress, and plan for tomorrow.
- Purpose: Ensure all loose ends are tied up and prepare for the next day.

5:00 PM – 6:00 PM: Exercise/Personal Time

- Activities: Engage in physical activity or personal hobbies.
- Purpose: Transition from work to personal life, maintaining balance and well-being.

Sample Weekend Day Schedule

7:00 AM – 8:00 AM: Leisurely Morning Routine

- Activities: Wake up, enjoy a relaxed breakfast, read, or meditate.
- Purpose: Start the day at a comfortable pace, focusing on relaxation.

8:00 AM – 10:00 AM: Personal Projects/Hobbies

- Activities: Work on a personal project or hobby or pursue creative interests.
- Purpose: Dedicate time to activities that bring joy and fulfillment.

10:00 AM – 12:00 PM: Household Chores/Errands

- Activities: Clean, organize, shop for groceries, or run errands.
- Purpose: Take care of household responsibilities and errands efficiently.

12:00 PM – 1:00 PM: Lunch with Family/Friends

- Activities: Enjoy a meal with loved ones or friends at home or out.
- Purpose: Foster connections and enjoy social time.

1:00 PM – 3:00 PM: Outdoor Activity/Exercise

- Activities: Go for a hike, bike ride, or other outdoor activities.
- Purpose: Spend time in nature, stay active, and enjoy fresh air.

3:00 PM – 5:00 PM: Relaxation/Free Time

- Activities: Read, watch a movie, nap, or engage in other leisure activities.
- Purpose: Unwind and recharge before the evening.

5:00 PM – 7:00 PM: Dinner and Evening Routine

- Activities: Prepare and enjoy dinner, followed by a relaxing evening routine.
- Purpose: Wind down and prepare for a restful night.

7:00 PM – 9:00 PM: Social Time/Entertainment

- ➤ Activities: Spend time with family and friends or enjoy entertainment (games, TV, etc.).
- ➤ Purpose: End the day with enjoyable social interactions or entertainment.

Sample Mixed Day Schedule (Work and Personal Commitments)

6:30 AM – 7:30 AM: Morning Routine

- ➢ Activities: Exercise, breakfast, and plan the day.
- ➢ Purpose: Start the day energized and prepared.

7:30 AM – 9:00 AM: Deep Work

- ➢ Activities: Focus on a critical work task (e.g., project development, writing).
- ➢ Purpose: Use early morning focus to accomplish important work tasks.

9:00 AM – 10:00 AM: Email and Communication

- ➢ Activities: Manage work emails and communications.
- ➢ Purpose: Clear the inbox and respond to necessary communications.

10:00 AM – 12:00 PM: Personal Errands/Tasks

- ➢ Activities: Run errands, attend appointments, or handle personal tasks.
- ➢ Purpose: Address personal responsibilities during a less demanding work period.

12:00 PM – 1:00 PM: Lunch Break

- ➢ Activities: Enjoy a meal, take a walk, or relax.
- ➢ Purpose: Recharge for the rest of the day.

1:00 PM – 3:00 PM: Meetings/Collaborative Work

- ➢ Activities: Participate in work meetings or collaborative sessions.
- ➢ Purpose: Engage in teamwork and communication.

3:00 PM – 4:00 PM: Personal Development

- ➢ Activities: Take an online course, read, or work on a skill.
- ➢ Purpose: Invest in personal growth and learning.

4:00 PM – 5:00 PM: Buffer Block/Wrap-Up

- ➢ Activities: Finalize work tasks, review the day, and plan for tomorrow.
- ➢ Purpose: Ensure all work is completed and prepare for the next day.

5:00 PM – 6:00 PM: Family Time/Evening Routine

- ➢ Activities: Spend time with family, have dinner, and wind down.
- ➢ Purpose: Transition from work to personal time, fostering relationships and relaxation.

These templates are just starting points— feel free to modify them to fit your specific needs and circumstances. The key to successful time blocking is to create a schedule that reflects your priorities and supports your goals while allowing for the flexibility needed to handle life's unpredictability.

www.ingramcontent.com/pod-product-compliance
Lightning Source LLC
Chambersburg PA
CBHW070351230526
45471CB00006B/2524